The Perfect Touch

Responding to the Voice of the Lord

by

Leslie Johnson

All scripture quotations are taken from the
Authorized King James Version of the Bible

Printed in the United States of America.

ISBN #1-58538-014-8

Leslie Johnson
𝕾pirit of 𝕻rophecy 𝕮hurch
P. O. Box 750234
Topeka, KS   66675

e-mail at lesliej@cjnetworks.com
Phone: 785/266-1112

Contents

The Perfect Touch

Chapter 1

I Almost Missed It!

Maybe you are wondering, is this book written for women on how to make the perfect fashion statement or have the perfect manicure? Well, my friend and personal nail lady, Ruby, does do the perfect ten, but this book is for all who want to know how to respond to *The Perfect Touch* from the Lord. I know that we all miss *The Perfect Touch*, the perfect moment, or the perfect Word from the Lord from time to time; and recently I discovered that missing *The Perfect Touch* from God would have not only been a great loss to me, but all of God's people to this Nation.

I love to praise and worship, and during that time at a recent Crusade my husband and I were directing, I discerned that the Lord desired to speak to His people. Many times praise and worship is a special time when the Holy Spirit will prompt us that He would like to speak through one of His servants. Over the years, this is an area I have asked the Lord to make me more sensitive to His Spirit and give me direction on who He would like to use as a willing vessel; to edify, exhort and comfort His people. The Lord knows that my heart is to keep me free to flow in His Spirit.

We have some great seasoned Prophets and Saints of God at these Crusades, and each meeting I would be talking with the Lord to see if He wanted to use one of us to speak to His people. To me, it is so much more important to hear the Word of the Lord than who is in charge of the microphone. However, I am aware and do understand that we need to keep things in order. We have that fine line to cross and need to be aware and use discernment. On that day in January, the two

5

prophets we had ministering at the Crusade with us, had not been given as much freedom with other ministries as with ours; therefore, they didn't always let me know that the Lord wanted to speak to His people unless I asked them. I had to be so sensitive to the Holy Spirit to know when to hand the microphone over to them.

This particular day, I knew that the Lord wanted to speak. I began to ask the Lord, "Does Gene or someone else have the Word from You?"

The Lord spoke to me and He told me to give the microphone to Gene. I said, "Lord, did I hear you right? You want me to give the microphone to Gene?"

He answered back to me, and said, "Yes."

You think that I would have responded right away and that would be all the Lord would have to say to me, but I went a step further and said, "But Lord, he is just standing there with his eyes closed, his hands are clasp together and he doesn't look like he has anything to say." I asked the Lord again. "You want me to give the microphone to Gene, right?"

Again His voice spoke to me and said, "Yes, Leslie, give the microphone to Gene. I have a Word to speak through him."

"Okay, gotcha Lord." And, oh, wow, what a Word from the Lord! It was so powerful and so awesome that I still find myself in awe of what the Lord said.

After the Word was given through Gene, a great reverence and fear of God came over me. I became aware more than ever of the awesome responsibility that God had placed on me. At that very moment, had I not responded, all of God's people of this nation would have missed the voice of the Lord. The Lord wasn't just speaking to us who were there at that meeting, or even at that special moment; but, it was a Word that all of God's people of this wonderful Country should hear. I realized, that at this specific moment in time, it was my responsibility to respond to His voice and hand over the microphone to another Saint of God. If I had missed the touch from the Lord to respond, we would have missed His anointing at that very moment and missed the Word from our King.

I wept, and cried out to the Lord, "Don't let me ever miss your prompting, your touch, your desire to speak to your people."

We, as Christians, have an awesome responsibility that we take for granted. We do not realize the importance of responding to the voice of the Lord. The Word of the Lord that came forth, that important day was given through one of God's Prophet's, Gene Bacon. This Word is for all of God's children.

The Word given to Gene is as follows: "I will provide for you," says the Lord. "I will do things that you thought could never be. I have greater things for you than what you see now, if you will continue. If you will persevere, you will prevail in the Spirit."

"Even the Kingdom of Heaven will be taken by force," says God. "My people should be raised up as a mighty army; walking hand in hand, walking in rank. The ranks will not be broken, walking together, united together. I say unto My people—as many as will hear My voice, that as many as will obey My Word—that I will use you in these days, powerfully," says God.

"Don't fear because of those sins that you've been dealing with, don't fear. Trust in Me. Those things you are dealing with, walk in the light. The blood of Jesus Christ will cleanse you from all of those sins. For I understand, they are but dust and that you still yet are flesh," says the Lord.

"I've said to you that you should forsake all of your sins, you should forsake all and follow after me. I want you to understand, My children, that I realize that you are not perfect. I want your hearts perfect before me—that you'd have a perfect heart before me. You would not sigh for those things you do

7

not have victory over. You will rejoice over your enemy and that you would defeat your enemy through your thanksgiving and your praise unto Me," says God.

"That you would stand before Me, and you would have the Sword of the Spirit—your weapon in your hand. You will go forth and you will defeat your enemy," says God. "I'm calling you to a place in Me. I'm calling you to a place by Me and I will draw you there. I will bring you there. I say unto you, that you do not need to do everything by yourselves, for I am there for you. I am there to help you. I'm there to heal you. I'm there to restore. I'm there to give back unto you that which the enemy has taken, that which he has stolen. I will give it back and I will restore it.

"Just as I spoke to my servant, Joshua, and I told him to walk through the land. Every place that the sole of his feet would tread upon, that I would give it unto him. Even so, I say this unto you, that every place that the sole of your feet would tread upon, I will give it unto you," says the Lord.

"I want you to understand some things that are taking place in these days. My Spirit, My anointing, the demonstration of My power is being poured out in your midst. There will be many righteous things done in this nation, and where there has been wickedness and unrighteousness I will restore and I will heal," says God. "I will bring righteousness again to this nation. I will bring a righteous people unto this nation. My people will walk as the brightness of the Son and in glory of their God. That glory will shine throughout this nation and the wicked will see it and they will rejoice in the Lord their God. They will come unto Me.

"I'm saying unto you now to let My light shine in you. To not snuff out that light, but to let that light shine perfectly and let it shine brightly. I want to say this unto you, that in this day that you're living in, there is a great work that needs to be done. There are many men and women who I am raising up as

8

a mighty army throughout this nation and other nations of the world."

The Lord says, "I want you to understand that there are some of you here, even this night, who I will give into your hand and I will give you the ability to get wealth. I am saying unto you now—those of you with a pure heart—if you will seek after Me, I will give unto you liberally. If you will give liberally unto Me, I will give liberally unto you. This is my promise, this is My Word to you. I don't want you to fear for those things you have need of. I don't want you to fear the finances for the work of the ministry. I will give you an abundance. I will give you more than enough. I will provide miraculously at times. I will give unto you everything that is needed and necessary for this harvest.

"I will give it and I want to remind you that I know that you are but dust. For I am your Maker, I am your Creator, I know you and understand you. I can be touched with the feelings of your infirmities and I have compassion upon you. I want you to know the great depths of my love for you. I am saying unto you that you will have victory in this day and this hour. You will go over this land, over this nation, and righteousness shall be restored unto this land," says God. "Where sin abounds, grace abounds the more. There's much sin in this nation, but My grace will abound so much more.

"I want you to look up and I want you to hold your heads up and not to be looking down and discouraged—not disappointed. I want you to be encouraged in Me and enlightened by My Word, enlightened by My Spirit. As many as will hear, as many as will obey, I will use you and I will send you. The nations need to hear the Word of the Lord. I am raising up a people in this nation that will go out into the nations of the world, like never before—in greater numbers than ever before.

"I have spoken unto some of your hearts and I have told you that I would send you unto the nations of the world, but you have not believed Me," says God. "You have not believed Me because you've not seen how that it could be done, but I say to you that I will do it. I say unto you be encouraged in Me, have faith in Me and if you will seek God, I will send you.

"You're going to see the young people in this land going, for they have a faith in Me and they put their trust unto Me. And you're going to see many young people going unto the nations of the world. You're going to see many of your youth being raised up in My Spirit—anointed and in power—and they'll go forth manifesting My Spirit and My power and My might. I'm raising up a generation of Joshua's, and they're ready. Their hearts are prepared and I've prepared a Moses generation. Those who will speak wisdom into the Joshua's, those who will give unto them. Those who will impart unto them," says the Lord.

"I am raising up a mighty work in this day, for I say unto you that even from the very beginning of this year I've started a new thing. A new thing and you will see it spring forth, it will not tarry but it will come, for this is the day. For the expectation I have had for this nation, this is the time that it will be brought forth. This is the time that my expectation for this nation will be fulfilled. This is the time that the wicked of this nation will be brought to me—they will be brought unto their knees. They will be converted unto Me and they will love Me with all their heart and they will serve Me. The wicked of this generation will so far outshine them that are saved now. I will provoke them unto jealousy by a people that were not a people, and by a people who did not know My name. I'll provoke them that are Mine," says God.

"I am saying to those who are mine that this is the day; this is the hour to take the Sword in your hand, the Word of the Lord, the Sword of the Spirit. This is the day to be matured in Me, this is the day to be complete in Me, for you have not yet a long time. For the time is short and the days are short. I'm doing a quick work and I will cut it short into righteousness. It will be cut short," says God.

"Ask for wisdom of Me to know your length of days. Ask wisdom of me to know your time in this life. Ask wisdom of Me to know the season and the time you're living in, I will give it unto you," says the Lord.

"I'm doing a work that will far exceed anything that the past generation and this generation has ever seen. For I am doing a righteous work, and a righteous work will spring forth through a righteous people. <u>I'm raising up a righteous nation, I am raising up a holy nation. As America was founded and established in righteousness, even so it shall return. It shall return unto righteousness. For just as I have not forgotten Israel as a nation, I have not forgotten America as a nation either. I will restore it. It will not be because of her righteousness, but it will be for My name sake,"</u> says God.

"I will restore in this nation, and I will give it My might and My Spirit. My power will be poured out into this nation. As many as will hear and as many as will obey. As many as will walk in the light of My Word, the revelation of My Word. I will raise them up in strength and they'll see My glory. You'll see visions and revelation of My glory that you've never seen before. I will unveil the heavens," says God.

"I will unveil My face—that you might look into My face and that you might see. As many as see My face, they will be changed and they will be delivered. For those of you who have been seeking Me and you've been praying, 'Oh God, I am so tired of the sinful flesh.' This is the day of deliverance. This is your day of glory," says the Lord. "This is the day you've been seeking for. This is the day you've been praying for and I will do great things in your midst and as many as will hear, I will use you." ...thus saith the Lord.

Let us realize that we all, God's children, have an awesome responsibility to respond to His voice. The Lord speaks to us, His children, all the time. We just need to learn to listen, obey and respond to Him. Our lives would be so much better and perfected if we would only listen, hear and obey that still small voice. All of Jesus's children, the ones who know Him, hear His voice. We just need to recognize that we have the capability to respond.

Psalms 95:7 *For he is our God; and we are the people of his pasture, and the sheep of his hand. To day if ye will hear his voice,*

John 10:3-5 *To him the porter openeth; and the sheep hear his voice: and he calleth his own sheep by name, and leadeth them out. And when he putteth forth his own sheep, he goeth before them, and the sheep follow him: for they know his voice. And a stranger will they not follow, but will flee from him: for they know not the voice of strangers.*

Acts 22:14 *And he said, The God of our fathers hath chosen thee, that thou shouldest know his will, and see that Just One, and shouldest hear the voice of his mouth*

After the meeting that night, I spoke to the prophets who were with us and begged them, "Please, please do not let me miss it. I fear missing the Lord speak. Please take the microphone and speak the Word of the Lord when He is prompting you."

The response that I was about to hear was a sad, shocking comment by one of the Prophets of the Lord that day. He said, "Leslie, we are used to being invited to speak in churches and other Christian events, and unless the microphone is handed to us, we are to be quiet."

I cried out to the Lord, "Oh Lord, let us hear your Prophets speak!"

Jeremiah 23:28 *The prophet that hath a dream, let him tell a dream; and he that hath my word, let him speak my word faithfully. What is the chaff to the wheat? saith the* **LORD.**

Some may think that it is a disadvantage in ministry if you have never been to Bible College. Well, my husband Stan and I have not been to Bible College. However, I do know that God is not interested in man elevating man. He is looking for faithful servants who will persevere. Just because God has called Stan and I to this ministry and now we are doing Crusades, does not make us "special". We are a very "normal" Christian family who desires to please our Lord and do what He tells us to do. Everyone of you who believe in the Lord Jesus Christ as your Lord, Savior and Master, have the capability to hear Him speak. Being filled and baptized in the Holy Spirit is a gift from the Lord, and helps us to become more in tune to Him. I truly believe that too many Christians are looking at leadership to hear the voice of the Lord, and not tuning into *The Perfect Touch* of God for themselves. You don't want to miss what the Lord is saying to you, do you? He has awesome plans for you and your family, your business, your life, and the ministry He has called and chosen for you.

Colossians 1:9 *For this cause we also, since the day we heard it, do not cease to pray for you, and to desire that ye might be filled with the knowledge of his will in all wisdom and spiritual understanding;*

After I realized how important it truly is to not miss what the Lord says, I asked the Lord that next week, every night before I went to bed, "Don't let me miss it!"

Within that same week, I had a dream. In the dream I saw a friend of mine. He showed me her face and then her

13

back. Her back was full of muscles. You know, muscles like a washboard tummy. The Lord began to speak to her that, "He made her strong in the natural, and now He was going to make her strong in spiritual warfare." In my dream, I then turned her around back towards me, and I began to speak a further Word of the Lord to her. While sleeping, all of a sudden I recognized the voice of the Lord, and jumped up out of bed and ran to get a piece of paper and pen. I was determined that I would not miss the anointing at that very moment and *The Perfect Touch* from Him. I began to write the Word of the Lord specifically to her.

Later that day, I faxed what the Lord had shown me in the dream and what I had received from the Holy Spirit. She called me back a few hours later and said, "You just don't know how much we needed that encouraging Word today. The Lord truly ministered to us. This Word from the Lord truly blessed us. We have been going through a trial, and I was wondering if the Lord even cared. I was wondering if He was here in the midst with us."

Jesus is so powerful, so wonderful, that we need to be obedient to His voice so that we can be an encourager to our friends and loved ones. The Lord again showed me something. He showed me that if I had just been lazy and decided to stay asleep, I would have missed the opportunity for my friend to receive *The Perfect Touch* of the Lord. The Lord is speaking to us all the time. This book is about responding to the voice of the Lord. He gives us direction, encouragement, plans, and just what we need at the right time, if we will just learn to recognize when Jesus is speaking to us.

Don't miss *The Perfect Touch* from the Lord. Respond when He speaks!

Chapter 2

The Perfect Rose

Several months prior to the writing of this book, a Word of the Lord came forth, and it was prophesied to me that I would be an author. The Lord said we would be publishing more books from new authors.

And then the prophet turned to me and said, "Leslie, you are one of the authors of several books. The first one, you need to get it written right away."

After the Word was spoken, Stan, my husband yelled out and said, "I knew it, I knew it, I knew it."

I'm thinking, "You knew what?"

Then Stan said, "And I even know the name of the book—*The Perfect Touch*!"

As soon as he said that, I also knew the name, *The Perfect Touch*. At that moment, the Lord took me back to a thought He had given me years prior. So, that is what the Lord has been wanting me to use this name for.

I have been hanging on to these particular three words for over a decade, wondering often, what are they for? These are just three simple words I would tell myself. Why, over the years, do they keep creeping up on me. I've tried several times using that phrase for different things that we would do; like having a dinner party and calling it *The Perfect Touch*, or having a gathering of my girlfriends over for a spa day. After the events I would still hunger about those three words. I knew that something special would be used for those three words, and the Lord also gave me a vision of a beautiful red rose. I could not get these three words, or the rose, out of my mind for years.

15

They would just not disappear. They continued to stay with me and I was always looking for the right thing. I even thought maybe I was to invent something, but knew deep in my heart there was something more important, more special down the road to use this phrase, *The Perfect Touch.*

Okay Lord, maybe you do want me to invent something, so this friend of mine and myself came up with this brilliant idea, so we thought. At the time we weren't so sure about getting oil on our hands when we were to pray for people. After all it is kind of messy, so we brainstormed and came up with a wonderful solution to the mess. I told her, "I know, we will get oil and put it in a little bottle with a roller in it. You know, like the roll-on deodorant? Let's add some frankincense and myrrh, and then all we would do is just roll the oil on the person's forehead. Now wouldn't that be so cool?"

However, we didn't patent that wonderful idea, but I know someone else has, because they now sell those bottles in Bible bookstores. I was going to call that invention *The Perfect Touch.* Man, maybe I've missed something! No, actually I now know the plan that the Lord had all along. It is just that sometimes, *The Perfect Touch,* doesn't come right away.

When the Word was given that I would be an author, immediately I knew the name of the book, and was also given a vision that night of what the cover of the book would be. I saw a white book with gold writing and a perfect rose. It was as if you could reach out and touch the rose. When I woke up the next morning I was so excited, because I had the book title and even the vision of what the cover was to look like. I am thinking, "This is great!"

And then all of a sudden I asked the Lord, "This is great Lord, but what about the middle of the book? You know, Lord, the words that go inside a book!" It seems the Lord works backwards with me. I have to know what the finished product looks like before I begin. In the natural I'm kind of that way. I need to know and see what the results are—to picture in my mind the finished product.

Later that day, my wonderful husband sent me a dozen red roses. On the card he wrote, "*The Perfect Touch*! With Love." As I was pondering, and in awe, that first of all I got a dozen red roses from my husband—for nothing! It wasn't even my birthday. Now all of us ladies can relate, that this kind of behavior from our husbands is absolutely *The Perfect Touch*, especially when I realized that he thought about me during the day.

After I sat and gazed at the beautiful roses, the Lord began to speak to me about a perfect rose. The petals of a rose are soft but firm, silky but coarse, textured yet smooth, brilliant in color, yet makes you feel as if the rose is a very delicate creation. The rose has thorns, yet they can be removed. The stem is hard to break, yet the leaves can be taken off easily. The rose is beautiful from the time of a bud to the full bloom. The smell is so spectacular that we want manufacturers to make perfume from the rose so we ladies will smell like one.

This is how our life is with Jesus. Our Lord can come to us softly and gently, yet firmly tug on our hearts to know Him. Our life with the Lord is like taking a road trip. This trip with the Lord can be bumpy in the flesh at times, yet when the perfect moment comes, it is like silk. It is like we slide right into where we needed to be all along. As our Savior smooths out the rough places in our lives, sometimes that sandpaper hurts, and sometimes we are stubborn to change. Sometimes we become set in our ways and say, "There is nothing wrong with me, I'm just fine. I'm just like He made me." We tend to forget that circumstances in our lives, and the sin we get into, make us who we are. We become like a stiff rod, we are not going to bend, not one little bit. However, as the Lord starts removing some of the useless things in our lives that He is not pleased with, we begin to blossom and then we bloom. As we

move from being a young bud, not ready to receive Him and His direction, we slowly open up to a full bloom. The Lord wants us to become that sweet smelling savor, like the rose. Jesus wants us to know the direction He has for us. He wants us to become aware of the plan He has for our lives. He wants us to totally yield to Him. When we are going the path that He has for us, then we can offer up that sweet smelling savor to our Lord.

Genesis 8:21 *And the LORD smelled a sweet savour; and the LORD said in his heart, I will not again curse the ground any more for man's sake; for the imagination of man's heart is evil from his youth; neither will I again smite any more every thing living, as I have done.*

Do you know His will for your life? We can and should know the Lord's will for ourselves.

Acts 22:14 *And he said, The God of our fathers hath chosen thee, that thou shouldest know his will, and see that Just One, and shouldest hear the voice of his mouth.*

Knowing His will for our lives is *The Perfect Touch* **from God.**

Chapter 3

Just Look Around

The Perfect Touch comes from the Lord in different ways. Have you ever experienced reading His Word, when all of a sudden, the perfect revelation knowledge comes to you? Sometimes as you are in prayer and supplication, the answer to the question you have, becomes so evident. We know it was Him, because we know of our weaknesses. We know that there is no possible way we could have in the natural figured that question out. Sometimes *The Perfect Touch* comes from a spoken word from a family member; a friend, a young child, spouse or even from one of God's other creations, the love of an animal. Have you ever experienced this? The Lord gives us answers to our questions and concerns all the time.

Looking out my back door early one evening before the sun went down, in a field across the road were about ten beautiful deer. I was overtaken by God's creation; the beautiful land, the beautiful deer family and how they were staying together. I have looked out that back door so many times, but the Lord was doing something very special for me at that very instance. The family of deer were very alert, but kept on grazing and following each other. If they made a quick move, they were able to keep their footing.

Just a few minutes beforehand, I was pondering with the Lord on some very specific things going on with our finances, ministry and family. The Lord shows us answers all the time, but many times we just have not come to realize when He is giving us the answers. If we begin to look around and become supernaturally aware, we will get the response to many of our

19

questions and concerns immediately. By watching this family of deer, the Lord began to answer my prayer I had taken to the throne room. He was showing me how the deer family were staying together and eating together, yet they were all very aware of their surroundings. The deer have great stability and balance on their feet and they are able to keep from falling because of this. They have great ability to jump over things and can run very fast, but they are always aware of their surroundings.

Psalms 18:29-36 *For by thee I have run through a troop; and by my God have I leaped over a wall. As for God, his way is perfect: the word of the LORD is tried: he is a buckler to all those that trust in him. For who is God save the LORD? or who is a rock save our God? It is God that girdeth me with strength, and maketh my way perfect. He maketh my feet like hinds' feet, and setteth me upon my high places. He teacheth my hands to war, so that a bow of steel is broken by mine arms. Thou hast also given me the shield of thy salvation: and thy right hand hath holden me up, and thy gentleness hath made me great. Thou hast enlarged my steps under me, that my feet did not slip.*

Jesus wants us to be strong and stable. He wants us to be aware of the evil going on around us, but we need to be able to dodge the bullet, so to speak, and to run or fight if we need to. The family of deer relied on each other and stayed together. There are times we need to jump over hurdles and run fast, and there are times just to graze. The enemy will come in to kill, steal and destroy so we need to stay alert. The enemy is looking for whom he may devour. Notice, he is looking for whom he may.

1 Peter 5:6 *Humble yourselves therefore under the mighty hand of God, that he may exalt you in due time:*

Casting all your care upon him; for he careth for you. Be sober, be <u>vigilant</u>; because your adversary the devil, as a roaring lion, walketh about, seeking whom he may <u>devour</u>: Whom resist stedfast in the faith, knowing that the same afflictions are accomplished in your brethren that are in the world. But the God of all grace, who hath called us unto his eternal glory by Christ Jesus, after that ye have suffered a while, make you perfect, stablish, strengthen, settle you. To him be glory and dominion for ever and ever. Amen.

I want to take a look at these verses very carefully. What does the word sober mean? Sober is to be self-controlled and keeping in balance. The word vigilant means staying watchful and alert to danger or trouble. Devour means to consume or destroy with a devastating force. The enemy is searching and looking for someone whom he can devour with a devastating force. Oh Lord, do not let us become that person the enemy is searching for. The Lord wants us to cast all of our care upon Him. He cares for us. Jesus will make us perfect, stablished, and strengthen us.

As I was pondering and just gazing at the deer, Jesus spoke to me with *The Perfect Touch* concerning my prayer to Him at that very moment. We, as a family, were to stay together and be very sure-footed. We are to be grounded in our faith and not stumble. The other thing He showed me was we needed to be very alert as to the enemy's tactics. We need to pray that supernaturally and through the gifts of the Holy Spirit, we will become more in tune with His voice. If we become aware, we can avoid being in the enemy's line of fire. We are not to hide, but we can fight in the spiritual arena even before it arrives in the natural.

Another thing God showed me at that moment, was how the deer family had joy. They were playing and frolicking around the great big field. Sure they could be right in the line of fire,

but they stayed alert and were having what looked like fun. Never have I seen deer so playful with each other, yet keeping an eye on their surroundings. Even through the battles of life, we need to always remember the only thing that can get us through circumstances of this life is the joy of the Lord. If we keep this in mind we can be grateful, happy, joyous people no matter what is going on in our life.

Nehemiah 8:10 *Then he said unto them, Go your way, eat the fat, and drink the sweet, and send portions unto them for whom nothing is prepared: for this day is holy unto our Lord: neither be ye sorry; <u>for the joy of the LORD is your strength.</u>*

I recently heard a minister of the Lord, whom I respect so very much, give a testimony of walking in the joy of the Lord at **all** times, in **all** things. One evening their house caught on fire. As the man and his wife were running outside, his wife was crying and yelling, "What are we going to do? What are we going to do?"

The man answered back, and said, "We are going to praise the Lord while we wait for the fire trucks to arrive."

His wife exclaimed, "What? Praise the Lord? But our house is on fire!"

They began to praise the Lord, and not under their breath or quietly—but loud! Don't you know that the neighbors, the firemen, and strangers passing by, must have thought they were nuts?! As they were praising the Lord, Jesus intervened at that instance. The Word says that He inhabits the praises of His people.

Psalms 22:3 *But thou art holy, O thou that inhabitest the praises of Israel.*

If we want the Lord to be there when things aren't going so wonderful, then we should be praising Him in **all** things. I want you to know that this couple had little damage and the things replaced ended up being better than what they had before. They didn't lose any of the memorable, important things in their life. The scriptures say we should praise the Lord in **all** things.

Psalms 34:1-4 *I will bless the LORD at <u>all</u> times: his praise shall continually be in my mouth. My soul shall make her boast in the LORD: the humble shall hear thereof, and be glad. O magnify the LORD with me, and let us exalt his name together. I sought the LORD, and he heard me, and delivered me from <u>all</u> my fears.*

When we praise the Lord, the scriptures say that the spirit of heaviness cannot stay around. How can depression and oppression stay in the midst of praising the Lord? It can't. If there is a time of despair in the your life, probably like me, the last thing you want to do is to feel better. We want to stay in our self-pity, depression, and stay in the pit. The devil will make us feel so unworthy to praise our Lord at those times. The reason he does is because he knows if we start praising the Lord, all of his little demons will have to leave. Those demons won't be able to continue to oppress us. Unless you are in total rebellion and keep taking your eyes off of the Lord, you can receive the joy of the Lord no matter what is going on in your life when you praise Him.

Isaiah 61:3 *To appoint unto them that mourn in Zion, to give unto them beauty for ashes, the oil of joy for mourning, the garment of praise for the spirit of heaviness; that they might be called trees of righteousness, the planting of the LORD, that he might be glorified.*

The Perfect Touch

This is *The Perfect Touch* of the Lord, keeping His joy.

Chapter 4

Where's the Love?

Believe it or not, the Lord will from time to time allow us to go through trials and tribulations. By going through these times, Jesus will begin to allow our flesh to be revealed. He will cause us to take a real good look at our hearts. Yuk! is usually what we see. We have recently gone through one of the toughest years of our lives. However, by keeping our hearts and minds focused on the joy of the Lord, we have such peace each day even though in the natural it seemed as if everything around us was falling apart. Our ministry was in deep financial trouble and in the spirit there was much fighting going on. The enemy was out to destroy us and the vision that God had given our ministry.

Would you believe we even had other spiritual leaders—Christian people—praying curses of death to us and our ministry? Now, where's the love in that? In the natural it was devastating. However, I knew in my spirit that we were to do the work of the Lord and if He wanted to change directions for the ministry, that was fine. I also knew He did not want death to occur to us, our family, finances, or especially the ministry that He had begun. If there was one thing I knew, it was most certainly, that the joy of the Lord would be my strength! It was a struggle some days, but, the Lord was faithful to give me strength as long as I praised Him and sought after His joy.

Too many times we Christians think that ministers of God should be perfect. I recently heard a well known woman of God talking about how she used to feel condemned each day on something she may have not handled properly the day before.

25

One thing that should be apparent, is that when we first accept Jesus as our Lord and Savior, we do not become perfect. We should continually strive to be righteous; live a holy life and continue to get closer to the Lord; and walk the walk toward holiness, righteousness and perfection. When we are first saved, we probably still continue to do more ungodly things instead of the new road of being righteous. Each day we should get a little closer toward walking righteously with the Lord. Before long, if we would look at our life, we would probably realize we are getting better about being doers of the Word instead of just hearers. (At least that is what should happen if we truly had an experience of salvation—a new birth.) Too many times we tend to look on the outward appearance of someone and not what is in their heart. We seem to judge all the things that a person is doing wrong in our eyes instead of the good work of the Lord they are doing. The Lord looks on our heart and ever so gently, yet firmly, changes those things that are not of Him.

I have seen and known people using the words, "thus saith the Lord" to get their own desires, will and vision instilled in other Christians. We as Christians need to start exhorting, lifting up, and becoming an encourager to each other. Oh Lord, let us not blame each other so freely.

Over the years we have observed our fellow brothers and sisters in Christ become very judgmental and critical of each other. Instead, don't you think we should pray for them to walk the walk the Lord has given them, and that their ministry would be on the right track with God? Too many times they just kill and destroy, in the Spirit, the life of a ministry that God birthed. We as Christians tend to forget that the Lord has called His people to minister in a variety of ways. He has given us diversities of gifts. Many times, just because we didn't like how a ministry did something, we cursed it instead of praying that the Lord would see that their ministry would stay on the right track.

Remember the children of Israel and how they were in the wilderness for forty years? Do you remember why they stayed in the wilderness? It was because of all of their complaining and murmuring. Murmuring and complaining can cause the blessings of the Lord to be stopped and hindered in your life. Not only can you cause jeopardy in another person's ministry by praying and complaining against them, but you will cause the blessings of God to be stopped in your own life. *The Perfect Touch* of the Lord from Christian to Christian should be of love - not hate, forgiving - not unforgiving, edifying - not tearing down, correction in love - not destroying, and praying - not condemning and cursing in prayer. Lord, let us become quick to hear, slow to speak, and quick to forgive. If we continue to walk in our own flesh and curse each other, how are we ever going to find unity with each other? We all see through a glass darkly and we have become the spiritual police with each other. I know that complaining, murmuring, cursing, gossiping and unforgiveness cannot be pleasing to the Lord. This is not His *Perfect Touch* in our lives.

I have a good friend, Jo Ann, a personal intercessor of mine who had a vision. I believe this is a Word for us Christians, that God wants us to become more Christ-like.

In Jo's vision, the Lord showed her a picture of a huge tree. She saw a gigantic trunk and a large array of branches growing from this trunk. On all the branches were thousands of cocoons. These cocoons represent us. The tree trunk is Jesus and the branches are His hands lifting us up. As we continue to pray in the Spirit, He will remove the dead flesh like nature removes the outer shell of the cocoon. As the outer shell falls off of the cocoon, a beautiful butterfly will make its presence known. God wants us to remove the dead flesh so we can emerge like the butterfly. He wants us to make our presence known unto Him through fervent prayer. We need to get the heart of Christ so we can pray blessings for each other and desire

27

to see the good things of the Lord come to our brothers and sisters in Christ. Instead of trying to get the dead flesh off of someone else, let's focus on our own lives with the Lord.

An important lesson I have learned and do not have total understanding of, is that our prayers are heard and answered whether they be of a good report or bad. As Christians, through our prayers, we can tear down and destroy a ministry someone has been given and destroy a fellow believer. Or, we can pray God's will and blessings in their life and see the fruit of the Spirit in them develop. It is up to us, believers in Christ, in a lot of respect. We, as God's people, need to realize that if our prayers have become the prayers of death, failure, and even praying God will destroy a fellow believer, they might be successful in that prayer being answered. However, the damage and curse will come back to the person praying that unrighteous prayer.

A true example we can share is exactly that. Another minister of the Lord was discouraged and disliked the ministry the Lord had given us, and in his mind we were not obeying the Word of the Lord. He was jealous of the position and authority God had given my husband and myself, and he was coveting the ministry God had us begin; however, we knew we were doing God's work to the best of our ability. This other ministry, his intercessors and anyone whom he could influence, began to pray a death curse to our ministry and even to us.

I couldn't believe it when I heard this man say directly from his mouth, "There is nothing you, Stan or Leslie, can do. God is going to destroy the ministry He has given you. Death will occur to the ministry and maybe even you." This prayer came from his heart. I began rebuking this statement and started praying...

Psalms 118:17 *I shall not die, but live, and declare the works of the LORD.*

As he began getting more of his team declaring words of death, we were getting more on our team declaring words of life. We, of course, prayed for his ministry and that the Lord would use his ministry for the works of the Lord.

You need to understand a very important aspect to this death threat that this minister of God spoke. There is power in the words you speak. You need to be very cautious of everything that comes out of your mouth.

A very unfortunate reversal to this man's ministry occurred. He cursed us with death, then he saw death happen in his own ministry. When we found out about the death of a fellow believer in his own ministry, we were very distraught. It was an awful feeling, and we knew this man of God had caused the curse to come back on him. We had great compassion for his ministry and the family of the lost loved one. This is a very important part the Lord wants us to grasp. There is power in the tongue.

Proverbs 18:21 *Death and life are in the power of the tongue: and they that love it shall eat the fruit thereof.*

When you pray in the Holy Spirit—in tongues—do not think you are praying the perfect prayer language - **unless your heart is right**. Our hearts must be clean before God to pray for people. Is your heart right when you are upset and angry with a loved one or friend? Many times you probably think, "I will just pray in the Spirit because I don't have the right words in my heart to pray right now." Where do you think the praying of tongues comes from? **It comes from your heart**. We are the temple of the Holy Spirit. If your heart is wrong you may be sending curses in your prayer language instead of edification to a person. Do not pray for anyone in the Spirit or from your heart until you make sure it is **clean and pure** before the Lord. It is often said these days that Christians fight Christians more than they do the enemy. We are the only "religion" that puts down and destroys one another ever so quickly.

Galatians 5:16-26 *This I say then, Walk in the Spirit, and ye shall not fulfil the lust of the flesh. For the flesh lusteth against the Spirit, and the Spirit against the flesh: and these are contrary the one to the other: so that ye cannot do the things that ye would. But if ye be led of the Spirit, ye are not under the law. Now the works of the flesh are manifest, which are these; Adultery, fornication, uncleanness, lasciviousness, Idolatry, witchcraft, hatred, variance, emulations, wrath, strife, seditions, heresies, Envyings, murders, drunkenness, revellings, and such like: of the which I tell you before, as I have also told you in time past, that they which do such things shall not inherit the kingdom of God. But the fruit of the Spirit is love, joy, peace, longsuffering, gentleness, goodness, faith, Meekness, temperance: against such there is no law. And they that are Christ's have crucified the flesh with the affections and lusts. If we live in the Spirit, let us also walk in the Spirit. Let us not be desirous of vain glory, provoking one another, envying one another.*

Remember *The Perfect Touch* is when you can reach out to someone with the love of Jesus whether it be another fellow Christian or an unbeliever. Don't get in to justifying your heart for doing something you think is right. The heart deceives us.

Jeremiah 17:9 *The heart is deceitful above all things, and desperately wicked: who can know it?*

We need to remember that if we have bitter envying and strife in our hearts, then this wisdom descends not from above, but is earthly, sensual, and from the devil. Wisdom from above is first pure, then peaceable, gentle and easy to be entreated, full of mercy and good fruits. Don't become so full of envy and strife that you allow jealousy and self-pity to become your fruit.

James 3:14-18 *But if ye have bitter envying and strife in your hearts, glory not, and lie not against the truth. This wisdom descendeth not from above, but is earthly, sensual, devilish. For where envying and strife is, there is confusion and every evil work. But the wisdom that is from above is first pure, then peaceable, gentle, and easy to be intreated, full of mercy and good fruits, without partiality, and without hypocrisy. And the fruit of righteousness is sown in peace of them that make peace.*

Remember sharing love is *The Perfect Touch* **of the Lord.**

The Perfect Touch

The Perfect Touch

Chapter 5

Ouch! That Hurt!

The devil has one up on us Christians. He has caused disputes to come against us from each other, sometimes in the most craftiest ways. One area, for example, that has become such a stupid area of disagreement between Christians, is whether the rapture will take place pre, mid, or post tribulation. Now that is something to argue about, don't you think? Of course not, there are scriptures that indicate each one of these beliefs could be the truth.

I have lived with a prophecy student for many years. I am married to the man whom God called to allow speakers to speak on Bible Prophecy. In seven years we hosted around one hundred speakers on Bible Prophecy. I have heard the best of them. One thing I can say about the hundred or so speakers is they rarely ever spoke about the rapture. There are too many other prophecies happening each day without getting into that debate. There are people who can show you scriptures to support all three positions. There are also scriptures which indicate there is not even a rapture - that there is a gathering and on we go into the millennium.

Does this argument give us the authority to tear someone down and cause an area of anger and disagreement? We need to all pray we have revelation knowledge and study the Word so that we may all know the truth of the Word. Let's pray that the Lord will reveal the mysteries of His Word to us all. We all know that the Lord will return when it is the right time. We are to watch and be aware of the season and times, but to dispute among us has gotten us nowhere. All we should be concerned with is—are we ready when the trumpet will sound? This should

33

be the question of the hour. Are you going to be found without spots and soil of sin? The rapture is just a small disagreement in the body of Christ. There are many more issues that need to be resolved. Let us all become willing disciples of Christ.

The work of the Lord is not just the man or woman behind the pulpit. Too many times we leave the work for someone else to do. We desire just to be fed and not to feed others. When we get our eyes on someone else doing the work of the Lord's ministry, we are not walking the walk the Word tells us to. How many people have you led to the Lord? How many people have you laid hands on to be healed? Have you been divorced? Have you hurt a spouse or one of your children? Have you hurt a fellow believer? Have you been studying the Word of God? Do you have self pleasures, rather than pleasing someone else? Do you have sexual sins? Have you taken the Lord's name in vain? Have you desired to see another ministry, or someone else fail? Do you have covetousness and greed in your heart? Do you desire to see someone in the ministry not have the pleasures of life you may have? For example; a nice home, car or vacation? Do you tithe and give an offering from each paycheck? Have you fervently prayed for your loved ones? Have you not asked forgiveness of a loved one because of pride? Of course, the list could go on. The Lord would ask these questions not to condemn, but to get us on the right track with Him. You see, *The Perfect Touch* of the Lord is not to destroy His people. Let us not allow pride to get between the people of God, whom He created, and love one another. Pray for Godly wisdom and direction for those you believe may not be hearing from God the right way.

1 Thessalonians 5:14-15 *Now we exhort you, brethren, warn them that are unruly, comfort the feebleminded, support the weak, be patient toward <u>all</u> men. See that none render evil for evil unto any man; but ever follow that which is good,* *both among yourselves, and to <u>all</u> men.*

In case you haven't noticed, I am a person who asks many, many questions of the Lord, and of my friends and family. I have always been this way. My dad use to say to me, "You ask me more questions than all of my teachers throughout my years of education." This is embarrassing because he had many years of education. He was an opthalmologist—an eye surgeon.

My husband, Stan, has what he thinks is a "cute" little saying. He says when we get to heaven, Jesus is going to introduce me to everyone and say, "This is Leslie." They will say "Who?" Jesus answers and says, "You know, the one who always asked so many questions." The reply of everyone is "OH! Of course! Hi! Leslie."

Even the other night I told Stan that I talked to God all night long. He said, "Well what did God say?"

I said, "Nothing, I was the one asking all the questions, I didn't give Him time to answer me." I tell you this only so that you know it is important to pray all the time.

1 Thessalonians 5:16-21 *Rejoice evermore. Pray without ceasing. In every thing give thanks: for this is the will of God in Christ Jesus concerning you. Quench not the Spirit. Despise not prophesyings. Prove all things; hold fast that which is good.*

Without ceasing—wow, what a goal! In my prayer life I do ask a lot of questions, and I know He will give me an answer. I am learning all the time how He answers me. He will always answer our questions, we just need to get in tune with what He is saying to us. I have asked the Lord to allow me to start seeing the answers to my questions all around me, and for Him to give me a confirmation concerning the responses I hear from Him. The Lord is faithful to do this because He loves us.

Sometimes I feel that His still small voice is sure enough still, and it most assuredly is small. I don't mind His voice being still and small, I just want to hear Him speaking to me more **CLEARLY**.

A while back, I decided to ask the Lord to start giving me confirmations in response to His voice. Also, I asked that He would help me recognize *The Perfect Touch* from Him.

While driving one Sunday morning to a Crusade we were conducting, I was asking the Lord if there was anything He would want me to share with His people on this last morning of the Crusade. In my Spirit I heard, "Yes, I would like for you to tell them something."

I said out loud, "Lord, what is it you would like for me to say to your people?"

He said, "Tell them, JUST DO IT!"

Only it wasn't the "Nike" ad! Immediately upon receiving this Word from the Lord, I looked and a confirmation—a witness came to me. On the license plate in front of me, it read, "Do It". Oh the joy I felt when I knew something so simple, yet so significant, was from the Lord. He gave me that confirmation instantly, and if we become aware and ask the Lord to help us to be more spiritually discerning, then He will continually give us that confirmation. Just like the deer family, they were so aware of the evil, as well as the signs of good around them. They found the field full of greens just for them and safely grazed.

How many times have we asked the Lord a question, opened our Bible and the answer was right before our eyes? He does this for us all the time. Pray for *The Perfect Touch* from the Lord, and that every answer to our questions the Lord speaks to us will be revealed and confirmed right before our eyes. How exciting this is, when we can know and hear the voice of the Lord so perfectly. *The Perfect Touch* of the Lord can come to us even in the middle of the night. Before going to bed each evening, I ask the Lord to speak to me on whatever He would like to, and also pray He will give me insight concerning the warnings of things to come and areas He would like for me personally to work on.

Oh, how we should desire to be more Christ-like, to become more like Him. We should desire to be Holy and blameless before our King—desire to hear, "Well done, thou good and faithful servant." He will be faithful to answer you, just be patient with yourself to learn and hear the voice of the Lord and be able to discern which dreams and visions are from the Lord. If there is a dream, then we need to ask for interpretation and get a second witness concerning the dream or vision.

Recently I had a dream from the Lord, and told two Prophets of God about the dream to make sure that first; was it from God and second; did I hear the Lord right on the interpretation of the dream? I have had so many dreams from the Lord, that I have learned how to interpret the dreams. It just takes time and patience. However, this particular dream was so intense that I wanted to make double sure I heard right.

In the dream, I was walking by a building that looked like an apartment building. I felt a strong desire to go into this place and knew that the Lord had called me to minister to someone specifically in there. Upon entering the apartment building, I found a young male child who needed a miracle from God. This apartment complex was a place where family members brought sick loved ones that needed extra help for a family member who was deathly ill. This young child captured my heart and I found myself taking care of him; feeding him, changing him, but most of all praying in the Spirit for him constantly. I then looked and noticed the little boy's mom, and was particularly drawn to the look on her face. You could tell she was very distraught and discouraged, and she had such a foul, mad look on her face. I asked the Lord, "What is wrong with her?"

He said, "She is very, very weary. This is why I have sent you here. She is very tired and mad at the situation of her child. She has cried many tears and she needs help."

Taking her by the hand I said, "I understand your pain and know that you are even very angry with God for your child's sickness. God sent me here to help you."

About that time, her little boy began crying in such pain and crawled upon his mothers lap. I looked at her face again, and as she looked at her little boy this time, she had such a peace come over her. You see, she knew that someone was sent there to help. She was rocking her little one back and forth, and I asked her, "How did your son get that way?"

She said, "The last fourteen days of my pregnancy I became very ill. I kept mentioning to the doctors that I was very concerned about my baby. I felt like the infection was passing from my blood to my unborn child and that my baby would be very sick. Sure enough when my baby was born, the infection had passed from me to my child. This infection affected his stomach and intestines—especially each time he eats—he becomes very ill and has a lot of pain. The disease he has is hema..." [I do not know the medical term for this. I just know that she said hema something.]

I then took the child in my arms, gave him a warm bath, prayed for him and got him to sleep. Still to this day, this child is on my heart daily to pray. I was so troubled all day long after this dream I kept searching the Lord. What was this? What did He want me to do with this dream? It was so real. I knew it was a powerful dream from the Lord and I couldn't get it off of my mind. Later in the day while praying, again I asked the Lord, "Lord, is this real? Was this a real child? Did you really send me there in Spirit?"

The Lord, said, "Yes, this is a real child and yes, you are called to intercede, and yes, I sent you there in the Spirit."

This may seem very far fetched to some of you, but when you have an experience like this, you know God is in control. He will do with us what He wants to do. I have asked the Lord more about this child. Now I intercede for him often, and have asked the Lord to let me visit him again to see the progress and even give me his name.

The Lord loves us so much that He will call strangers amongst us to intercede on our behalf. Maybe someday I will actually get to meet this family in the natural. I know the Lord is going to heal this little one completely. To become aware and know that my Lord actually trusted me enough to intercede for him and his family is an honor for which I am truly grateful. I praise the Lord that He kept this dream on my mind so strongly, and that I pressed in on God until I received an answer. I could have very easily just dismissed this dream as something foolish.

Many times the dreams and visions we have are for us personally, but we try and make them for all those in our life and for all people to hear. At our ministry we receive hundreds of dreams and visions from people who desire us to put them in our newsletter, on the radio, or even let them be on television. Did it ever occur to them that God had a plan for them to do the work themselves? We are a selfish bunch of people who desire that others do the work and not do it ourselves. Many times a person will not do what they have been asked, then leave that ministry and walk away, never to help them again financially, prayerfully, or giving of any help whatsoever. We also do this with our own family. It's easier to leave them than to pray and work things out. Unfortunately, we have become a selfish bunch of lukewarm Christians. Oh Lord, let us become your people, with a need to see that the work of Your ministry gets done.

Many Christian organizations are suffering because we, as believers, have left our post and left God. We hold on to the things of life and our own desires instead of giving of our tithe and offerings unto the work of the Lord. God took our ministry through a transition—from one direction to another. Instead of staying loyal, many people dropped their support in the most critical time of need. Many of God's people just step on and destroy each other instead of help get the work of the Lord back on track and support each other.

In prayer, I have asked the Lord, "What do you want us to do to help our ministry grow and be a great lifeline to your people?"

He spoke to me very clearly, "I want you to give your way out of the hole you are in." We have begun to see the necessity and work the Lord has called different ministries. We support them by giving a tithe each and every day. The Lord is faithful to us if we are faithful to Him and what He tells us to do.

The first week that we were going to give a tenth each day, we decided to give it at the end of the week. However, the Lord spoke to me very clearly and said, "I told you to give each day. The enemy will come in with a plan, to make an emergency, so that you cannot give of your tithe this week." Unfortunately, we ignored this Word from the Lord and sure enough, we did not obey and give daily. To our surprise, (yea, right!), the enemy came in with a plan of destruction, and the tenth of the week did not go to help another ministry. The Lord let us learn a lesson. Give daily of the tithe and the enemy will not have a chance to come in and take it away. We need to do this in every area of our life. We desire *The Perfect Touch* of the Lord, but we do not want to give back. Why don't we become the people of the Lord and give of ourselves to help each other and not tear down each other? Sometimes the things in the natural, like financial problems, health problems, marital problems and family matters, make it hard to have the faith.

Hebrews 11:1 *Now faith is the substance of things hoped for, the evidence of things not seen.*

Faith is the substance of things hoped for, and the evidence of the things not seen. We need to believe and thank the Lord before our request arrives. Faith is a substance. It is real, we can know even before we see it. This is why we need to be careful when the Lord speaks to us. If we react too soon then it can be destructive. Faith always is in action before we see it in the natural. As we realize the faith in action, then we can learn to become patient for the fulfillment of the faith-filled prayer and promise from God.

Let us become like that rose. Allow the Lord to grow in us to be one of His chosen beautiful people. Start over if needed and become just a bud, ready to grow into a beautiful full grown blossom of the beautiful rose. Be strong like the stem—rooted in the soil of righteousness. As the stem grows and becomes strong, allow the thorns to be removed one by one. The Holy Spirit will correct and reprove those things in our lives if we allow Him to. Removing the things of the flesh that are not pleasing to the Lord is sometimes painful. However, He will gently, yet firmly, remove those things that are not desired of Him. The thorns in our sides can be removed. Do not be rebellious to keep the ungodly things in our lives. The prick of the thorn hurts us, as well as others we are in contact with. Become a sweet smelling savor like the rose. You want to be found sweet smelling in the natural, as well as the spiritual with the Lord's people. Cleanse yourself daily in the natural as well as in the spiritual. We need to become like a beautiful rose with the Lord using us with *The Perfect Touch*. The rose can be brilliant in color, as well as soft in color. How and when do we present ourselves boldly or softly must be the Lord's leading and not our own. Don't be so easily offended and get your leaves knocked off when things don't go your way. Even though the rose is beautiful when the thorns are removed, the smell still strong and the color so brilliant, the rose is a very delicate creation. We, as God's people, are delicate also. We become

41

easily offended, carrying our burdens and not giving them to our Creator, and we desire to get even with others. Lord, let us become like-minded people who care deeply for each other. Help us to give *The Perfect Touch*!

The Lord will remove the thorns if we allow Him to.

Chapter 6

Wake Me Up Lord

Hearing and receiving the voice of the Lord is sometimes a task that seems too far to reach. In times past, the Lord seemed too far to answer me and make everything better. When you are going through trials and tribulations, He can seem so far away. The first thing to do is make sure your heart is pure, and that your sins are forgiven. Make sure there is no guile in your life, because sin will sure hinder you from hearing the Lord speak. Don't justify your actions, ask the Lord to correct you where you need to be corrected.

Changing our personality is sometimes not in our equation. We desire to be the same ungodly person we were when we first became born again. We bring our unkept closet and excess baggage along with us, and as we grow closer to the Lord, we then begin to clean out our closet and get rid of the baggage that is not pleasing to our Lord.

There is one thing I wanted more than anything in my life, and that was to have the power of God. I wanted to become so sensitive to His Spirit, that I would be able to respond when He spoke. I wanted to be clean and righteous. I've often thought, "Lord, as I am getting rid of the sin in my life, will I be able to hear you better?" Of course, as we make that decision to walk a righteous walk, we can continue to hear Him more clearly.

One thing I have done and continue to do is ask the Lord to wake me up at certain times. Hating to be awakened by music or especially a loud buzzing sound, I prefer that my Lord, my maker, ever so gently awake me. This is also what my family prefers, if you know what I mean. By learning to hear the voice of the Lord waking me up each day, then I could tune into His sound, His voice, His presence and learn to hear when He is speaking to me. Because of this training of tuning in, when I hear Him, I respond. When unsure whether the voice is of the Lord, wait and get a confirmation.

Many times just because we feel comfortable or uncomfortable about a person, situation, or a voice we hear, this does not necessarily mean it is from God. Sometimes it is and sometimes it is not. For example, Stan and I had been married for about a year when we moved from our hometown. In those early days of marriage, we began our search for a good church. The first church we attended was a Unity Church. The people were nice, there was so much "love" and good words spoken; however, there was no Jesus—at least not the true one and only Lord Jesus Christ, our God and King. They felt that everyone has good in them and all people were going to heaven, no matter what religion they were.

Of course, we know this is incorrect. As we walked into the building, I was so overcome with laughter in that place— unfortunately, the snorting kind of laughter. The more I tried to sustain, the more I snorted and laughed out loud. As they were singing, "Let there be peace on earth", I laughed even harder. The first thing the Pastor announced was he was resigning. I started laughing out loud uncontrollably, but this time, even louder. As a matter of fact, I was laughing so hard that I was crying. Stan kept nudging me to stop, and the laughter just got stronger and stronger, louder and louder, as well as the snorting.

As you can guess, their service was very short that day. You can imagine all the strange looks I got. Stan was embarrassed so much that there was no way he would ever go back to that "church". Praise the Lord! I now realize that the Spirit of God was on me. This place was the epitome of how the enemy has deceived so many. It was a joke. The people believed the lie that they were gods—they thought they were so good. They thought they could save themselves, just by singing peace and visualizing good. What a lie we buy into!

Romans 8:2-8 *For the law of the Spirit of life in Christ Jesus hath made me free from the law of sin and death. For what the law could not do, in that it was weak through the flesh, God sending his own Son in the likeness of sinful flesh, and for sin, condemned sin in the flesh: That the righteousness of the law might be fulfilled in us, who walk not after the flesh, but after the Spirit. For they that are after the flesh do mind the things of the flesh; but they that are after the Spirit the things of the Spirit. For to be carnally minded is death; but to be spiritually minded is life and peace. Because the carnal mind is enmity against God: for it is not subject to the law of God, neither indeed can be. So then they that are in the flesh cannot please God.*

Another Sunday we visited a "Spirit-filled Church". The music was alive and they were clapping and dancing. I thought this was wonderful! After only about two minutes, Stan turned to me and said, "Are you ready to go?"

I said, "No!"

However, being the "submissive" wife I am, we immediately left. That church was on fire for the Lord and we left. Shame on us! However, the Lord had different plans for us. Hallelujah! Just because we were uncomfortable in a church did not mean we were hearing from the Lord that these people were of the devil. As a matter of fact, it was quite the opposite. Later we discovered that church was one of the best Spirit-filled churches in the area. Learn to hear the voice of the Lord, so that He can keep us on the right track. Now after being Spirit-filled for over two decades; we are on fire, Spirit-filled, tongue talking, clapping hands, dancing people for our most Holy King. It is so wonderful giving your all to the Lord!

To hear from the Lord, we must become a humble spirit. Giving our all to Jesus during daily prayer, praise and worship will enable us to know the presence of the Lord and hear Him. Many of us want to hear the Lord's voice and be used of Him in ministry—without giving of ourselves. Let me ask you a question. If you do not spend time with the Lord in prayer, praise and worship, how do you expect to hear Him when He speaks, and how can you feel His presence? Communication is a two-way thing. We want it all to be our way, or the highway!

Reading and studying the Word of the Lord, the Bible, you can hear the voice of the Lord. However, the Word is very clear that it says in **2 Timothy 3:7** *Ever learning, and never able to come to the knowledge of the truth.* We need to keep things in balance. There is life in the Spirit of God.

John 6:63 *It is the spirit that quickeneth; the flesh profiteth nothing: the words that I speak unto you, they are spirit, and they are life.*

2 Corinthians 3:6 *Who also hath made us able ministers of the new testament; not of the letter, but of the spirit: for the letter killeth, but the spirit giveth life.*

The Perfect Touch of the Lord comes when we can spend time with Him and He with us. You may be wondering about, "How do I make the time? This season in my life is so hectic with children, work, being a taxi, or trying to do the work of the Lord, that I just do not know if I can find the time."

The Lord is very aware of our situations and the season of life we are in. When my children were small, I would be scrubbing the kitchen floor and be praying and waiting on the Lord. He was always faithful to answer. I would be driving around town taking my daughter to one of her many endeavors, praying and asking for Him to speak to me. He was always faithful.

We can always justify that, "I do not have the time to spend with the Lord". Aren't we grateful He doesn't say the same thing back to us? We all need to find the perfect place to spend time with the Lord.

My most favorite place to spend with the Lord, and where I ask many questions is in my prayer closet—the bathtub. The quiet time alone with the Lord is wonderful and I can ask as many questions as I want and He will answer me. Don't find an excuse, just take the time.

Our son, Shawn, is a romantic type of guy. He says he likes making photograph images of himself and Jesus at different places. Shawn likes to go where it is just himself and the Lord. He has climbed to the top of a mountain and arrived just before sunrise to spend time with the Lord. He goes to a rose garden often. During the summer, Shawn will sit on a lawn chair as the sun is going down, just spending time with the Lord. He says it is like making a scrapbook of just himself and the Lord. He says that he can see, in his mind, that the Lord has His hand around him and they are watching that sunrise, sunset, or the beautiful surrounding together. He says, "Mom, I have communication going on between me and my Lord."

The Lord is faithful to show up wherever you may be. I know the Lord will give many confirmations when you have heard that still small voice. Now that's *The Perfect Touch!*

Another way to hear the voice of the Lord is through dreams and visions. Throughout the Bible Jesus spoke in parables. He was constantly giving us examples of life to learn from. Many times a dream or vision is a parable trying to figure the puzzle out. When you are given a dream, ask the Lord first if the dream was from Him. If the dream was from the Lord, ask to receive the dream again. It is important to get up and write the dream down immediately, because you don't want to be like me in the past, and fool yourself to think that you will remember the dream later on that day. After you write the dream down, ask the Lord for the interpretation of the dream. Again, write the dream down to receive the interpretation. Always get a second opinion about the dream to check and see if it was from God; and second, is the interpretation from God? This is a check we should keep in our lives. Sometimes a dream is for us personally, or for our family. Other times it is for whole fellowships to receive and share with others. As you continue hearing from the Lord, by dreams, you will learn to discern which dreams are for you personally, versus for all of God's people to hear. Realize sometimes you may have a dream and hear a similar dream on the radio, etc. Take this as a confirmation the Lord is wanting you to prepare and pray.

A dream I received personally just for myself from the Lord, a personal touch from Him, was several years ago. My dad had just past away, and I asked the Lord, "Please give me a confirmation that my dad is with you." I desired so deeply for the Lord to do this, even though several years beforehand, I had the opportunity to make sure my dad knew Jesus as his Lord and Savior, I still needed more reassurance.

Our God is so wonderful to give us the desires of our hearts. Within several months of my dad's death, a dream came to me one night about him. I had a great relationship with my dad, and was a real daddy's girl. I always loved to climb upon his lap, no matter how old I got. In this dream I climbed upon my dad's lap, and as I sat upon his big cuddly lap, I didn't say anything for a little bit because I found myself just staring in his eyes. As I continued to stare, I began to visit with him. We began to laugh and hug, but all the while I was drawn to his eyes. As I looked deep through the glasses he was wearing, I noticed something very different about my dad. I said, "Dad, your eyes, they are so beautiful. They are gold, pure gold, clear gold. Your pupils, they look like diamonds. They are the most beautiful diamonds I have ever seen—so brilliant, so bright, so clear."

My dad held me tight in his arms and he said to me, "Leslie, when you someday look upon these streets of pure gold, your eyes will look like mine. The reflection of what I see here is so awesome, so beautiful, no words can express. The streets of gold are so bright, so transparent, so pure the reflection is radiated from my eyes. The jewels are so perfect and so bright." He said all of this with such a peace and love that I knew where he was. He was walking the streets of gold!

Revelation 21:18-21 *And the building of the wall of it was of jasper: and the city was* <u>*pure gold, like unto clear glass*</u>*. And the foundations of the wall of the city were garnished with all manner of precious stones. The first foundation was jasper; the second, sapphire; the third, a chalcedony; the fourth, an emerald; The fifth, sardonyx; the sixth, sardius; the seventh, chrysolyte; the eighth, beryl; the ninth, a topaz; the tenth, a chrysoprasus; the eleventh, a jacinth; the twelfth, an amethyst. And the twelve gates were twelve pearls: every several gate was of one pearl: and the street of the city was* <u>*pure gold, as it were transparent glass*</u>*.*

This was a dream, just personally for me, from the Lord. He answered my question in such a vivid way as to never, ever forget. I would never doubt again where my dad was. He was with my soon coming King! I know now, beyond a shadow of doubt, that one day we will be together again. The Lord gave me a special version of *The Perfect Touch* just from Him. I felt so honored that my Lord would answer my question in such a special way from Himself, just to me. He will do the same for all of His children.

We as the children of God are not perfect. You know, even our children are not perfect, but the fear of the Lord can become evident in each of their lives. When Shawn was eighteen, he became, as most of you parents know the syndrome, "I'm an adult now because I am eighteen." Nevertheless, Shawn was about to learn a great big lesson in trying to outsmart God. The week prior to his eighteenth birthday, I began asking Shawn, "What are you wanting to do for your birthday?"

His remark was always the same. He would say, "Oh, my friends and I are going out to eat and probably go to a movie. I won't be home until late because we are going to go to the late movie—probably."

I would get an uneasy feeling each time I would ask Shawn, so I began praying and interceding, and asking the Lord questions. My question to the Lord was, "Where is Shawn and his friends really going? What are they going to do?"

Finally, the day of July 12th came. That morning the Lord spoke to me very clearly and said, "Shawn and his friends are going to Lawrence. They are going to go to (the Lord gave me the name) a dance hall and bar where they will let eighteen year-old's in." Shawn's friends showed up at our house, right on schedule. As Shawn came in to me to say good-bye I asked him again, "Shawn, where are you all going? What are you going to do?"

His comment once again was, "Oh! We are just going out to eat and probably go a movie." Shawn was about to receive a big surprise!

I said to him, "That is not what the Lord told me you were going to do."

At that moment you should have seen the look on his face when he realized that his sin had found him out. I told him exactly what the Lord had said; where he was really going, what they were really planning, and what they were really going to do. Shawn turned completely white. He learned a great big lesson on his eighteenth birthday that neither one of us will ever forget. As a matter of fact, Shawn has helped put the fear of God in our other two children, because he knows it is not worth the sin and it is sure not fun being found out.

Another lesson Shawn learned that night was probably even a harder one. I said to him, "Now you are going to march in there, in the other room where your friends are and apologize and repent for being such a bad example." I told him, "You are a leader. They respect your belief and walk with the Lord, and they look to you for guidance."

Here he was a young man, who just turned eighteen, a real man, and he had to go humble himself right there in front of his friends. Oh, did I mention that his friends were also told to leave the house and that he was grounded from going anywhere on his eighteenth birthday? The famous quote, "Oh what a web we weave when we purpose to deceive."

As Christian parents, we need to hear the voice of the Lord. We need His guidance and direction and so do our children. Our Lord loves us so much he does not want us to fail. He doesn't want us or our children to fail and fall into the jaws of Satan to be devoured. Ask the Lord to help you. He will give you insight—the insight to your children's hearts. I would much rather *The Perfect Touch* come from the Lord and not the evil, devastating touch from the enemy.

This story was not told to embarrass my son, because so far in his short life on this earth, he has kept very clean. He is a blessing to many and to our family. This story is revealed, first to let you know that not one of us is holy and righteous enough. It is a decision and walk each of us must desire to walk in daily. Praying for our loved ones, praying that our closets are clean, praying that our sins will be found out so each of us will walk holy before our Lord and King. Even though it was a tough lesson, Shawn had *The Perfect Touch* from his Lord. His Savior protected him from being devoured by the enemy.

Dreams come to us for direction, correction, and also warnings and events of the future. After going through several months of real burdens from our ministry, the Lord gave me a dream. Stan and I were on a huge ship. This ship was a beautiful ship with large windows all around. All of a sudden the ship ran into a heavy duty storm and was in turmoil. The largest waves I could have ever imagined, were slapping hard against this big vessel. As the waves hit the boat Stan and I were tossed around so much that our footing kept coming out from under us. We continued to cry out, "The blood of Jesus, The blood of Jesus!" My husband and I weren't scared, we just weren't quite sure as to what was happening.

As we looked out the windows, which were all around the ship, we saw a huge rock. It became quite obvious that we were about to hit this huge rock. As we got closer, we braced ourselves and hung on tight. The ship began to turn in order to avoid the crash, but sure enough, boom! We hit the rock and the ship began to turn upside down and sink. Stan and I, as well as others, were falling downward fast. In our minds we thought, "This is it! We are going to die. We are going to sink and drown." Then all of a sudden the ship stopped going downward. It didn't sink past a certain point. We caught ourselves and began to pull ourselves up to the top of the ship. As we were climbing up, I could see the big windows that were all around us. I looked out the windows and noticed that the reason the ship did not sink any further was that it was stuck upon that huge rock.

As I began to wake up from the dream, at first was very shaken thinking, "Oh no!, our ministry is done with. We are going to sink. We will live through it, but are we going to make it?"

I asked the Lord to give me the interpretation and what He said to me was so precious. He let me know that yes, it seemed we were on a downward spiral; however, He was that huge rock we landed on. He said, "I will protect you and that we would not sink." Hallelujah! The Lord said, "I will help you climb back up to the top, and I will guide the ship." He also said, "The ministry I have given you, I am just causing it to go in a different direction. As you make the turn, there is always a rough spot, but I will guide and direct the ship, for you were founded upon the rock."

All I could say to Him was, " Thank you, Lord. We will be faithful to do what you call us to do."

Psalms 18:2 *The LORD is my rock, and my fortress, and my deliverer; my God, my strength, in whom I will trust; my buckler, and the horn of my salvation, and my high tower.*

Psalms 62:2 *He only is my rock and my salvation he is my defence; I shall not be greatly moved.*

Psalms 62:6-7 *He only is my rock and my salvation: he is my defence; I shall not be moved. In God is my salvation and my glory: the rock of my strength, and my refuge, is in God.*

Psalms 89:26 *He shall cry unto me, Thou art my father, my God, and the rock of my salvation.*

Psalms 95:1 *O come, let us sing unto the LORD: let us make a joyful noise to the rock of our salvation.*

The Lord speaks to us through dreams to give us direction and promises. *The Perfect Touch* is a promise from the Lord that is very personal.

The following is a dream I received for the Body of Christ: At *The Power of Jesus Crusade!*, Stan and I were in the front row. There were many people attending, perhaps 1,000 people or more. During the praise and worship all of us noticed a waterfall flowing from heaven. It was coming through the ceiling of the building we were in. Everyone was focused on this massive waterfall. It was massive—bigger than Niagra

Falls, but it was a smooth flow of water. The strange thing about this massive waterfall was there was no sound of water, only a beautiful sound. It was not threatening, it was gentle, yet we knew the strength it had. We were not concerned with it coming in and filling the room to drown us. We were excited that it was there. There was such a peace on all of us, yet we all had a feeling of expectancy.

The water was flowing down on the crowd, yet we were desiring even more of God, more of His Spirit and power.

Looking up as far as I could see, I noticed the top of the waterfall going around an object. Looking closer, I could see it was going around what looked like a big chair. It seemed strange that it was going around the chair, the flow felt so strong. It was powerful and the water was flowing around us, yet we still wanted more.

We all began to pray and praise the Lord even more. We were all singing in unison a beautiful flowing song—a song never heard before. We were all singing the words in unity together, such as: Majesty, Glory, Honor, Beautiful, Lovely, Magnificent! We were singing the attributes of God.

Then the waterfall burst open! A burst of power, similar to a meteor shower or a ball of lightening, came directly from the throne of God. (This burst of power looked similar to when God wrote the Ten Commandments in the movie.) The burst of power shot across the room and hit one of the couples praising the Lord. It hit them so hard that it knocked them back and they were slain in the Spirit of God. Many of us ran over to them. The power was so strong, and at first we wondered if they would even survive this awesome touch of God. When they finally sat up, we noticed the woman had a mark of a dove impressed into her cheek just below the eye. We then turned and looked up at the top of the waterfall. Now the water was also flowing over and from the chair. Then we realized it wasn't just a chair, it was the throne of God!

As the water flowed over the throne, we could see the shape of it. When we realized that the water was also flowing from the throne of God, and not just a chair, we became very excited. A great reverent fear of God came over all of us. It was a gigantic throne and the waterfall was massive.

When we first saw the waterfall it was coming from heaven, but now, even more power came when the water also flowed over the throne.

As I began to wake up, the Lord kept telling me to get up. He wanted me to write this dream down and that He would begin to tell me more as I wrote it. I told the Lord, "Please don't make me get up, I just want to stay in your presence." This was such an awesome, powerful feeling. I felt like melted butter. I finally got up to write the dream.

The Lord said, "In times past My people have only seen a glimpse of what I am about to do. You were in the river, the flow, but you had to learn how to experience a small flow before I could give more of My power. If the flow had come directly from My throne you would have been swept away. My people were not ready to receive the most powerful flow. In times past the flow was only touching My throne. It was just touching the hem of My garment. Very shortly, as your desire for My power increases, and you press into Me with your praise, worship and determination, you will see My true power."

The Lord said, "My people have not been ready for this great outpouring, but you will soon experience a great and mighty outpouring amongst you and you will truly say, 'This Was God!'"

This power will only be explained as coming from God. It did not come because of what one of the ministers said, or anything His people did. God just decided to pour His virtue out more powerfully at *The Power of Jesus Crusades!*. He will touch some as they sit in their seat. He said that He will touch the whole arena, not just the ones in the front row.

The Lord told me that **NO ONE HAS EVER SEEN THIS KIND OF GLORY!** Other groups, as well as ours, have only seen and felt a small portion of what He is about to do. They thought they saw His power, they thought they saw His Glory, but they have NOT seen it yet!

Some believers hear the voice of the Lord through a vision. A dream is when you are asleep and a vision is when you are awake. When prophesying to people, many times the Lord will give me a vision of something. Sometimes it seems quite strange, but as I begin sharing the vision He is always there to show up and give the interpretation. Some believers receive a very detailed vision with a message to God's people. I for one, am very grateful for these visions, as they give me direction and correction for my life or the lives of others to whom I am ministering to. I know some believe that visions from God do not exist anymore, but the Word of the Lord says,

Hebrews 13:8 *Jesus is the same yesterday, today, and forever.*

I had a vision not long ago. In the vision, I saw a ladder and I believe this vision could be for each one of us. It was not just for the congregation at the time, but for all who are not taking the next step up. In the vision, a person was climbing the ladder. Their feet were moving up the ladder and their hands were grabbing the next step, but there was something wrong. As the vision progressed, everything that this person was doing was right, except the ladder was sideways. They were climbing sideways instead of going up the ladder. The Lord spoke and said, "This is how my people are. They are doing what I have asked them to do, but they are not progressing to the next level. My people have become stagnant and comfortable where they are. I want My people to strive to the next level, the next realm of faith, the next call I have for them. I have great works for

56

them to do and I do not want them to stay where they are."

Don't we as Christians do this? We get saved and become on fire for Jesus a little while. Then we get filled with the Lord's baptism and we become excited to work for the Lord, for a time. During other situations in our lives we fight the enemy hard, but only for a season. After a period of time goes by, we tend to let our guard down and become just hearers of the Word only. We think we are doing great works for the Lord, but in reality, spiritually we are going nowhere.

Remember, the Lord will awaken you, with His *Perfect Touch,* **just ask!**

The Perfect Touch

Chapter 7

Reaching Out and Touching Someone

Did you know that you could hear the Lord speak by listening to someone else? My husband says the way to hear from the Lord is television, telegraph and tellawoman. I say, "Stan, if you will just listen to me, then so many things in our life would be better. And, I wouldn't have to say I told you so." Amen, women? Many times I have asked the Lord a question and later found myself listening to something on the television or the radio, when all of a sudden, something they said answered that very question. Most likely, the Lord was telling me all along and I just wasn't listening. He had to get me to hear Him from listening to someone else.

An example in my life happened after my first son was adopted by my second husband, Stan. I would often asked the Lord, "Why did my ex-husband allow Stan to adopt Shawn?" This was kind of a funny question, because actually I was very grateful and happy that Stan adopted Shawn. However, being full of questions, as usual, I still wanted an answer.

The Lord allowed me to hear the answer from speaking with a young woman whom I didn't know very well. She was telling me how she and her husband were thinking about adopting a child. Somehow, we got on the subject of what to say to the child when he got old enough to know he had been adopted. I told her that Stan had adopted Shawn and she said to me, "Your ex-husband must have loved Shawn so much, that he let him go." That was it! I knew as soon as I heard it. The Lord was speaking through that young woman and she didn't even know it. Our Lord Jesus is so wonderful!

If we would just think about it, there are so many examples of the Lord speaking to us. Sometimes we are in a hurry, trying to get out the door quickly, and to our surprise as we are leaving, we forget something we need. We go back into the house and get the items we need—then the phone rings. As you answer the phone, you think, 'Oh no, it's my mom.' "Mom, I'll call you later," as she continues to tell you just one more thing... and then you go on your way.

As you get to the main intersection, not far from your house, there is a major wreck that just took place. If you had been there just minutes, or even seconds earlier, you would have been involved in that accident.

The Lord will allow whatever it takes to get our attention. If we had been listening and tuned into the Lord, we probably wouldn't have tried to leave when we originally wanted to. As a matter of fact, mom wouldn't have had to call. Wouldn't it be great if we could hear His voice so clear, and realize that our intercession for someone is more important than being on time?

A good listener is hard to find. Now these days, even when talking on the phone we are so preoccupied. I don't know how I survived before there were cordless phones for our houses, cell phones for our cars, and most importantly, caller ID. What wonderful inventions! Unfortunately, while talking with someone, they do not usually get our full attention anymore. We can wash dishes, make the bed, start the laundry, drive our child to dance, pick up groceries in the store—all the while talking on the phone. We have gotten even further away from being a good listener to those who need us. However, by becoming a good listener, this will help us to hear what the Lord is saying to us.

I am always telling my children, "Your sins will find

you out, so stay clean or the Lord will let me know what you are up to."

Psalms 69:5 *O God, thou knowest my foolishness; and my sins are not hid from thee.*

Proverbs 28:13 *He that covereth his sins shall not prosper: but whoso confesseth and forsaketh them shall have mercy.*

We should pray daily for Godly Supernatural Spiritual awareness and also natural awareness. This enables us to be led of the Holy Spirit and in the natural become aware of what is going on around us. My children know that we are listening to remarks from other people to see if there is any correction we need to make with them. We know that tough love is sometimes an important discipline that our children need from time to time, and discipline is a requirement from God. We are born in sin, and children soon learn good from evil.

I have a friend who has a six month old baby, Eryn. Eryn scooted over to some items on the floor. She started to reach for some electrical cords and immediately her mom clapped and yelled, "NO!" Eryn looked up at her mom, and as she was keeping an eye on her mom, she began to reach for the cords again. We don't realize that because of early discipline from our sinful nature we are born into, we can know what is right from wrong at a very early age. Sometimes it is important for you to be *The Perfect Touch* in someone's life.

There was a couple in our congregation who were having a hard time financially. They are very private people so they would not mention this to anyone. They decided they would pray to God, that He would intervene and supply all their needs. As fellow brothers and sisters in Christ, we should be able to spiritually discern when one of our fellow servants in our midst

61

is needing assistance. However, we are usually so caught up in our own troubles that we do not pay attention and listen to the Lord. Even in the natural, if we would pay attention, sometimes it is just a look on a face, that enables us to know what is going on in a person's life. I spoke to some of the leaders in our church regarding this couple and how I felt that they needed help financially. They agreed and said that the Lord was speaking to them also. As leaders of the church, we were so relieved that we listened to the Lord, because this couple was truly blessed. The Lord had responded and answered their prayer. However, if we had not responded to the voice of the Lord, they would have suffered needlessly. Become *The Perfect Touch* in someone's life.

Many times, as Christians, we look the other way and desire someone else to help our brothers and sisters in need. Recently I came across someone just like this. She mentioned that one of the leaders of another fellowship needed to go and help an older gentleman, whom she knew, get an air conditioner. She was angry because the leader didn't get to the older gentleman as quickly as she thought he should. Instead of taking the initiative to help this man herself, she just murmured and complained, stirring up trouble in that fellowship. This lady wanted to put the burden that the Lord had laid on her heart to someone else. Why do we do this? Instead, why don't we decide to help them ourselves? This lady was quick to point the finger at someone else and put the blame on the other person, when perhaps the Lord was speaking directly to her to help this man. Don't give someone else a burden when the Lord has given that burden to you. Too many times we want to delegate the situation to another Christian. If you are going to be responsible enough to delegate, then be prepared that it might not happen in your timing, or how you think it should be done.

God is preparing His people to be equipped and trained for the work of the ministry. That means not just the ministries

on the radio, television, or behind the pulpit are the only ones
doing the work of the Lord. That means you and me. We cry
out to God, "Please use me for your work and give me a
ministry." Look what happens next. When He gives us work
to do, but it is not quite what we want it to be, we complain,
and in turn, we become unfruitful and unfaithful to our Lord.

The ministry of helps is probably the most important
ministry for God's people. Hearing from the Lord and being
willing just to help is so important. Jesus was the greatest servant
of all. Helping and serving others is a great reward. He will
test you in the little things, and your heart, before you will be
given something big to do for Him. When you find something,
do it as unto the Lord.

Ecclesiastes 9:10 *Whatsoever thy hand findeth to do,
do it with thy might; for there is no work, nor device, nor
knowledge, nor wisdom, in the grave, whither thou goest.*

If we did not help each other, we would be a mess.
Maybe this is why our Country is in such disarray and ungodly.
What do you think? Too many of us, children of our Lord and
Savior, think that we are doing what the Lord wants us to.

Look, some of you go to church each Sunday, or at least
three times a year—whether you like it or not. Do you really
think the Lord wants you to be just pew warmers? Or better
yet, thinking yourself Godly because you make an appearance
once in a while. Just think what could happen in your fellowship
if everyone would hear the voice of the Lord and would do the
work God has called them to do. What an awesome church
fellowship that would be! However, some of you are saying, "I
would work in the church, but my Pastor will not let me."

Sometimes a person is too radical for the leaders of the
church to allow them to minister. Just calm down and begin
slowly. Sometimes you may need to find another fellowship to

go to - a fellowship where you can share your gifts. But there is one thing that you need to realize, in any fellowship that is of God, they will test and try you first before releasing you to minister to the Pastor's sheep. You might be required to teach the children's Sunday School first, when actually you only want to teach adults. You must prove your commitment and time, as well as knowing the Word, before a church will allow you to teach adults. This is just wisdom.

Another way to get practice and see if you are ready for teaching, is something we do at our church. We have a Friday night fellowship where we allow church members, who have a message on their heart, to share it with the congregation. This is our training and equipping night. Sometimes the leadership will have to visit with them later concerning some issues of their teaching, but that is all part of the growing and learning experience. If you will let the leadership of your church fellowship know you are interested in helping out in any area, they will, I promise, be so happy. They will find work for you to do. It might be cleaning the bathrooms for a while, but when you are doing this as unto the Lord, you can have joy. The Lord will be faithful to you.

A great mentor of mine, who is very strong in her gift of helps, knows this is her calling and chosen work for the Lord. She is a great teacher, as well as a great preacher. Because she knows the main gift God has for her, she is always receiving food, clothing, Bibles, etc., to give away and help others. She has put many miles on many vehicles for the Lord. God has always been faithful to get her where she is needed. When someone is in need, Lord, let us be quick to respond and help.

Have you ever noticed in most churches it is usually only a couple of people who do the work? If you haven't noticed, then it is probably because you are one who never helps with anything. We have a couple in our church, who without a doubt, have heard the voice of the Lord. They are always there when the doors are opened. This couple is always making sure the bathrooms are stocked, things are cleaned up, encouraging others, and overseeing that everything is running smoothly. They are also one of the best tithers we have. They are vital to our fellowship and we know we can count on them. This couple desires to hear and obey God so much that they will do whatever it takes to help. They haven't become great leaders or speakers for our church, but everyone knows they are priceless. They have such joy in their hearts and a peace about them. They know that everything they do and give of themselves, the Lord will repay. I know in their hearts they want to be used in the ministry; praying for people, laying on hands, counselling, and used out on the road in Crusades. You see, they want to be used of the Lord. They are servants of the most high King.

Jesus gave us a good example of being a servant. Jesus, our Lord and Savior, King of kings, Lord of lords, our God, He washed the disciples feet. He showed us the greatest gift we could offer is to be to be a servant of our Lord to His people. All too often, today's leaders have lifted themselves higher than the Lord, or they have allowed others to exalt and lift them high. In actuality, they should be the best example of a servant. Remember great things and moves of God start off little. When you are faithful in the not so noticeable things, He will be faithful to you in the bigger things of ministry. Hang in there! Do not be discouraged. Hearing the voice of the Lord and finding the work that is needed in your fellowship is very important. He shows up no matter what you are doing. God is no respecter of persons.

Acts 10:34 *Then Peter opened his mouth, and said, Of a truth I perceive that God is no respecter of persons:*

You see *The Perfect Touch* **of God is not always in the limelight.**

65

The Perfect Touch

Chapter 8

I Heard Him Speak

Some people hear the voice of the Lord through an audible voice. So far, I have not heard an audible voice from the Lord; however, the men and women of God who have heard an audible voice have experienced great tribulation. I tell people, "Be careful what you ask for. You might just receive what you ask for and discover it is not all the glitter and glamour you thought it was going to be." A friend of mine has prayed for years that her husband be a good provider—the breadwinner of the family. Presently he has been given a great opportunity and good wages, but along with this package was a move. Moving to another city, much less another state, was not in her plans. We need to make sure what we are praying for, and then, receive the blessings the way the Lord has planned for us.

There are many who desire and receive this special gift from the Lord, of hearing Him audibly. Personally, I would rather be tuned into the Lord in order to hear that still small voice and obey Him. To me, this is the greater challenge. If we can become a good listener when the Lord softly speaks to us, He wouldn't have to YELL!

Another way to hear the voice of the Lord is through His Prophets. Many times in our own personal lives we have been directed by Prophets of God. Sometimes we have received a word we really did not want to hear and thought, "Oh well, he is just human and he missed that part." Then suddenly, we realize we should have paid attention because things are happening exactly the way the prophet said it would, and we're thinking, "Man, couldn't he have been mistaken just a little bit?"

God **does** have a plan for each one of us. Sometimes, for us to become what He wants us to be, we have to go through various trials. From personal experience, I can tell you that these trials are not fun, but who said working for the Lord is always fun? It is a lot of work, but I wouldn't want any other boss.

Prophets are sent to us to direct us and give us the message of the Lord. We can make a decision to follow His plan or not. Since my husband and I have been called into the ministry, I have found out that for some reason, many believe that if you work for the Lord, it is all so very easy—it is like laying in a bed of beautiful roses. Many people think if you work for the Lord, chances are you get to travel, you only have to speak behind the pulpit one day a week, you may even get to pray for someone, you might get to watch video tapes and read books all day. Of course, I am being facetious. Let me tell you, when you hear from the Lord, to do the work of the ministry, He expects you to work hard. After many weeks of travelling, a vacation to me is just getting to stay home and sleep in my own bed. God is not a forty hour week boss, He expects you to be there when He says. He wants you to do more. There is no retirement in the ministry with God, until you go home to be with Him. God is a demanding boss; however, when there is rest, He is so faithful and so wonderful to repay and give you *The Perfect Touch* at its best! Hallelujah!

Being a prophet is a lonely, heart wrenching call on a life. Many have asked the Lord for this calling. Again, be careful of what you ask. When you finally walk in the office of a Prophet, there are times the words you must give are not fun. Prophets are very rejected much of the time and they are a peculiar people. I know, because the Lord has called me to be a prophetess. And, I am sure many would call me peculiar! A prophet must be bold to speak the truth and there is only black and white with them—this is wrong, or this is right! Prophets can be wrong sometimes. We need to realize the humanness side of our being. There have been times I have been wrong. Either I heard wrong, or thought the Lord was saying something else. I have had prophets speak a word to me and knew it was incorrect; however, I still took it to the throne room of God and checked it out. Prophets need to be very careful that they do not put their own twist on the Word of the Lord. There have been times in my own life when a young prophet, early in his call and having not heard properly from the Lord at all; will speak an evil, rebuking word, all the while trying to be humble and present it in love. If you don't run things from the Lord through His filter, then much damage can come to a person's life. I know, because it has happened to me. I had to decide to let the offense go and move on with my life in the Lord. I do praise God for the direction and voice of the Lord working through mature prophets in our lives. We have been able to know the direction, calling, change, and encouragement from prophets.

As prophets we must give the Word of the Lord in love. Many times a strong discipline from the Lord has come to Stan and I. However, the mature prophet gave the message in love and we knew exactly what the Word from God meant. Many prophets have been kicked out of churches, homes, families, and shunned from society. Often the reason is they do not minister in love, or are immature in their call.

A true prophet can sometimes be a coward—look at Elijah. He ran when Jezebel was after him. Another example, why didn't Jehu get rid of Jezebel? Why did it become the job of the eunuchs to push her out of the window? Prophets need to have compassion and walk in love. They must speak the Word of the Lord. Sometimes it is hard, but with the Lord's grace and much practice, a prophet can speak to a person's heart and do it with compassion. Like numerous things in ministry and life, it takes practice. Believe me, the best preachers out there have practiced their sermons over and over again to get them perfected as powerful messages. When we first begin to walk in the office of a Prophet, many times we are like babes. We make mistakes and sometimes we fall. The other five-fold ministers are given grace and mercy, and so should a prophet also be given the same grace and mercy. The other five-fold ministers; the Evangelist, the Teacher, the Apostle, the Pastor, all have a season to mature. They are all given a chance to practice. They are all given patience and mercy from the Saints of God. This same grace and mercy should be given for the Prophets.

Remember, a person receiving a prophecy should not be quick to judge the person giving it. In the same manner, the one prophesying should be careful with this gift. Also, just because you prophesy, this does not mean that you are a prophet. The Word says that we should all prophesy. Through experience, all prophets begin as intercessors and prayer warriors. As a matter of fact, there is no way one can be a true Prophet of God unless they are an intercessor first. Prophets must spend a lot of time in prayer and communicating with God. Don't you think as prophets, who give a Word from the Lord, should spend time hearing His voice in order to recognize His voice? Believe me, if you have a calling on your life to be a prophet, but do not desire to spend time with the Lord in prayer, your ministry will be short-lived. Your prophesying will become harder to give and you will not be accurate.

A Prophet of God should love to praise our Creator. The reason being, the Lord inhabits the praises of His people. If you and I desire to have the Lord with us when we prophesy, then we must praise Him. Many times I have seen a prophet try to walk in their own strength instead of God's anointing.

God gives us wisdom and there are times we need to rest. Men, yes, I am speaking especially to you. You are probably much worse than women when it comes to taking a rest from the ministry. You are conquerors, and you think you are men of steel. You think you can go forever. Unfortunately, you still have a body in which you inhabit, and until that body is resurrected, you will be limited in your strength. Prophets remember, to receive *The Perfect Touch* from the Lord when prophesying, you must walk in His wisdom and in His strength, not your own. If you do this, then you can prophesy accurately and become *The Perfect Touch* to someone else.

As a caution: Does this mean that everyone who gives personal prophecy's are called to be a prophet? The answer is no and absolutely NO! The Word says that we are all to prophesy.

1 Corinthians 13:9 *For we know in part, and we prophesy in part.*

1 Corinthians 14:31 *For ye may all prophesy one by one, that all may learn, and all may be comforted.*

However, the Word says some were called to be prophets. A prophet is under the divine guidance of God. A prophet is called to speak a future Word of encouragement, direction, and plan of the Lord. Prophets are people who hate error and deception. In other words, they judge what is right or what is wrong. They have a strong desire to see those things of God stay that way. If someone falls off the chalk line, they are quick to let them know. It is hard for them to keep quiet when they see evil around them taking place—they want to devour the enemy quickly. Prophets despise evil in a stronger way than most. The reason being, many times they have discernment and see the evil lurking before others even suspect it. This is one reason why prophets are disliked. They speak their mind before many are ready to receive. They are also able, through obviously the Lord's gift to them, to see people for who they really are in Christ. They know the heart of a person very

71

quickly. Their job is to warn other Christians, to warn cities and countries, and to help guide the churches in the right direction. You can see why so many Christian Fellowships have kicked the prophets out of the church. Our heart deceives us and we do not desire truth.

Finally, hearing the voice of the Lord through angel visitations. Again, I have not experienced a visitation from an angel that I could physically see. Personally, I believe a conversation from a true visitation of an Angel of the Lord is extremely rare. From scriptures and hearing from men and women of God, who have proven to me that they are telling the truth and are servants of Jesus Christ, they fell on their face and many could not get up or even look up. The scriptures tell us to not be afraid, but our righteousness, or lack of, will surely be revealed to us at that moment.

It is unfortunate that some have made a mockery out of an experience with an angel, causing many to believe that angels from God would not come and speak to us today. Believers know there is a devil, they know there are demons and believe they are still around. Let me ask you a question. Just what is a demon or Lucifer? They are fallen angels. So then, if there are fallen angels, don't you think that there are Angels of the Lord?

Some people have claimed to experience communication with fallen angels of light and have taken them as friends. In fact, we had experienced this in our church not long ago. A man, who called himself a prophet, said that he spoke to an Angel of the Lord. He said that this angel and he were friends, and the angel would tell him things. Unfortunately, this man was very deceived. He had not experienced being born again with the Lord. Jesus was not his Lord and Savior, and he believed that **all** people could find the road to Heaven, regardless of what religion they are. The fallen angels—the demons—had become his friends. He had gotten off into areas the Word of the Lord forbids us to go. For example, out of body experience and channeling. He was walking around with familiar spirits, and this man felt very special that they would come to him. My theory is because of his being rejected most of his life, he found a friend from the dark-side. Unfortunately, when faced with the truth and shown the error in speaking with these fallen angels, he would not turn to Jesus. Instead of taking loving correction and making his decision to accept the Lord as his Savior, he was very reluctant to give up his "friends".

One thing that is prominent with those who have had a true visitation from an Angel of the Lord, is one of total humility and many on their face before God. Not once have I ran across someone with a true Angel of Lord visitation end up with an "angel friend". Remember, we are to test the Spirits whether they be of God. I will say, just because they believe in Jesus, does not give the final authority that an angel be of God. Even the devil himself believes in Jesus and knows the Word of God. This is why he is seeking whom he can devour. You should test and try the Spirits. Test their fruit. Is this angel trying to take you places where God forbids in His Word? Are they telling you to speak death to someone? Are they coming to visit with anger? Are they coming to visit and complain of things going on in the world? Are they coming to visit and spend time with you just for the fun of it? Test and try the Spirits. A true visitation from one of the Lord's Angels, in which you communicate, would be *The Perfect Touch* from the Lord, and not likely to be forgotten.

If we could see in the spiritual realm, I am sure that we would become aware of all the visitations from angels in our lives. I had an experience and received *The Perfect Touch* from an Angel of the Lord. My daughter and I were on our way to the office and it was the first snowy day of the year. As I backed out of the driveway, I felt an urgency to pray. Even though there was fresh snow falling, the conditions of the road didn't look that bad. As we traveled down the road, it became icy and very slick. Continuing on towards the office, I was praying all the time, as the car didn't feel secure on this slick stretch of road. In a matter of seconds my car began to swerve back and forth. I tried to turn the car towards the direction of the swerve, but it didn't respond. The car was on its own path. At this point, everything seemed to move in slow motion. Leslie Ann and I just started crying out, "The Blood of Jesus, The Blood of Jesus!" Looking in front of me, there were two vehicles coming towards us from the opposite direction, and there was nothing I could do. We were swerving into the oncoming lane. As I continued to try and get control of the car, the two vehicles were getting closer. There was a small car approaching us and right behind the small car was a big, huge suburban! I had never realized how big those vehicles could look! Nevertheless, the car and the suburban were coming directly toward us. By continuing to stay on the path we were headed, I perceived the small car was going to miss us. Knowing this should have comforted me, but guess what? That BIG vehicle was going to broadside us. As we cried out to the Lord I knew there was nothing I could do, so I closed my eyes and just waited for the collision. I kept thinking, "The suburban is really going to hit us!" All of a sudden, my car just stopped. To my surprise when I opened my eyes, we were facing in the opposite direction. Looking in the rearview mirror to see when we were going to be hit, again to my surprise, there was no suburban. I looked in front of me and saw the smaller car, so I turned around and looked behind me again. Would you believe it, to my amazement, there still was no suburban! It just disappeared. I started yelling, "HALLELUJAH! HALLELUJAH! THANK YOU LORD!" My daughter and I started laughing, crying and shouting, "Thank you Lord, Thank you!"

I made my way to the office and told some of the employees about what had happened. At that moment, one of our employees, who was pregnant at the time, was waiting to be taken home by a gentleman from our office since the roads were slick. She was standing outside on the steps for him to drive up, when she looked down and saw two sets of footprints on the fresh fallen snow. As she looked, she notice that one set of footprints were very large and appeared to have no shoes on. She started laughing and thought, "Leslie walked in the office barefoot through the snow." Then all of a sudden, she realized that my feet were not that big. Then she thought, "Maybe Leslie Ann walked in the office barefoot." She looked in my car and saw that Leslie Ann was still in the car. As she gazed further at the footprints, she saw that my shoeprint was small, and a larger footprint was next to each step I took; however, the footprint was the imprint of a barefoot. She began to laugh and told the gentleman who was picking her up what she saw.

He said, "It seems as if Leslie's angel is big and barefoot."

You may think this is strange, but before I got out of the car there was fresh fallen snow, and absolutely no one had stepped one foot on it. Leslie Ann, my daughter, was still in the car, so they knew it wasn't her, and besides, her feet at that time were smaller than mine. I believe on that day my Guardian Angel removed the BIG suburban to prevent it from hitting us and causing damage. Not only was my angel barefoot, but he is big and strong! My appointed Guardian Angel kept me on the road and brought my car to a stop. Not only that, he picked up that big vehicle and placed it somewhere else. (Don't you know how weird those people must have felt when all of a sudden they realized they were on another stretch of road?) The angel even followed me into the office so I wouldn't fall. Isn't our Lord so awesome—that He would send His ministering angels to us and for us? We pray daily for the Lord's Angels to be with us and protect us. I know the Lord intervenes and prevents terrible experiences in our lives. Now I'd say that is *The Perfect Touch*!

The Perfect Touch

Remember, walk in Wisdom, Discernment, and Truth to prevent the fall and keep His *Perfect Touch*.

Chapter 9

Little Bundles of Joy

*D*id you know that you can receive *The Perfect Touch* from family? God allows loved ones in our lives to minister to us. He uses these special people to touch us right where we need it the most, at the most precious times, and always in His perfect timing.

When my son, Bentley, was just two years old, the Lord used that little hand of his to give me *The Perfect Touch*. I was carrying a basket of laundry down a flight of stairs at our home, when all of a sudden, I lost my footing and went tumbling down the stairs. Bentley heard me scream and he ran as fast as his little feet would let him. He asked, "Mommy, mommy, you okay?"

I didn't want to scare the little guy, but I was hurting real bad. I said, "Bentley, just pray for mommy. Mommy has a hurt."

Children learn all too well, don't they? Bentley quickly put his little hands on me (he had that part right) and said, "Dear fodder, tank you for dis food." Those words were so cute and they caught me off guard. I began laughing so hysterically that I forgot all about the aches and pains. The Lord answered that prayer from His little one, even though his words weren't exactly right. The Lord knew his heart. He wanted his mommy all better. I was healed instantly on the spot. I received *The Perfect Touch* from the Lord through a two year old. Remember, our children learn through example.

When Bentley was six years old, he received a word of wisdom and a word of knowledge for a friend of ours. At this time, we had a young lady staying with us. She had been in a car wreck and had broken her foot, so we were taking care of her. Bentley had just gotten off the school bus and came walking in the house. As he came in the house, I acknowledged him and bent down to get ready for my afternoon hug, but he just kept walking and passed me by. I thought this was really strange, so I followed him. He went straight into Stan's office where this young lady was, and spoke to her a few words from the Lord. Bentley said to her, "Jesus told me to come in here and to tell you that He is healing your foot right now. And if you will not elevate it and put it down, the circulation will return and your foot will be healed." He then turned around and said, "Hi mom!" and gave me a big hug. Wow! I didn't even think he knew what some of those words meant, and where in the world did that come from? Obviously, the young lady and I knew exactly where it came from. The Lord used one of His small servants to give this young woman *The Perfect Touch* of the Lord. Her foot was healed instantly and she had no problems after that. Praise the Lord!

Bentley is a young Apostle in training for the Lord, and still to this day, has a great anointing. He is full of compassion and love for people. Sometimes when Bentley gets a strong Word from the Lord for people, he just weeps. He is a young man full of knowledge and wisdom—a young man with many gifts from the Lord. The gifts in this child are just bottled up, ready to be made known at any moment—gifts in music, voice, prophesying, and especially in the mechanical things in life. Bentley has become my *Perfect Touch* for all appliances such as: setting of clocks on coffee makers and alarm clocks, computer problems, cell phones and remote controls. Anything mechanical, he's my man!!! He has *The Perfect Touch*, and he can pray for me anytime!

Sometimes our children will try to get what they want by using their cute little personalities, or manipulate you with their great big beautiful eyes. Sometimes the correction from the parent has to come in and give *The Perfect Touch*. Oh how our children will try to get away with things. This is what the Lord says of us—we, His children, do the same. Some children try to test your keenness not only in the spiritual, but also in the natural.

My stepson, Bryan, would try to get away with things often. He usually could because of those big, beautiful green puppy dog eyes. He knew he could just look at me and win me over. However, I was about to give him *The Perfect Touch* of a parent. When Bryan was ten years old, I had to take Shawn to a morning appointment. Bryan talked me into letting him stay at home alone because he was old enough. Before I left, Bryan said to me, "Can I have the leftover spaghetti for breakfast?" He loved spaghetti and would eat it all day long if he could.

Answering him I said, "No, we are going to eat it later because I won't have time to fix anything else. Besides that, it is breakfast time, so you should eat breakfast." When I arrived home, I looked at Bryan and said, "You ate spaghetti for breakfast, didn't you?"

Man, the look on his face! He was so surprised. He asked, "How did you know? I put everything up. I washed the bowl and I even brushed my teeth. How did you know?"

Still to this day I have not given him my secret. Moms just seem to have that special *Perfect Touch* from the Lord to know what is going on. We have keen eyesight, smell, and can outrun any child, no matter what age we are! One of the greatest gift's from God is intuition. Children especially can't hide from a Spirit-filled, discerning and praying mom.

Some children have a gift to radiate joy. That is my son, Shawn. He has always been able to give me such joy and bring about laughter. Even when he was a very young child, he had a way of making people laugh and be happy. He has that touch of joy in him that is contagious. Shawn is able to see joy, beauty, happiness, and the Lord at work in all things. People with this gift become a stable force in life. Being around a calm, cool personality to lull the storm around you is a real blessing. There are so many stories I could tell you about Shawn, but that would be a book in itself; however, there is one I would like to share.

You see, Shawn had a call on his life at a very early age. Stan and I led Shawn to the Lord when he was eight years old. At that time we were having Bible studies in our home. One evening Shawn made a definite decision to follow Jesus, and became an Evangelist at a very young age.

Several years later I was visiting with the school bus driver at the end of the school year. She made a comment to me, and said, "Well, I think Shawn almost has them all!" When she said this, there must have been a startled look on my face, because I was almost fearful to ask her what in the world was she talking about. I was kind of afraid to find out. By the look on my face, she knew I had no idea what she was talking about. She proceeded to tell me that each morning on the way to school, and then each afternoon on the way home from school, Shawn would preach to the other children on the bus. He would lead child by child to the Lord during the year. The bus lady was a Christian, so she was excited to see what would happen each day. She would pray daily that the Lord would give Shawn wisdom and know exactly what to say. Each day Shawn would take his Bible with him to school, to his classrooms and wherever he went. Here it was, the end of the school year and I had no idea what was going on the whole year on that school bus and at school. Not every child on the school bus accepted Jesus that year; however, they got the gospel given to them the whole year. Years later I have wondered how many are serving Jesus as their Lord and King, Master and Savior due to Shawn's evangelism.

Many friends from school came to respect Shawn

because of his belief in God. I always got wonderful reviews from his teachers. Their comments were always the same. Shawn is such a blessing. He always comes in the room with a smile on his face. He always has an encouraging word to give me and others. They were actually glad he brought his Bible each day because they could see a difference not only in Shawn, but also the classmates were better behaved when Shawn was around. Everyone just seems to like this young man.

When Shawn was sixteen, he worked for a movie theatre. After a little while, we noticed he seemed to become more like the world because of working there. Stan and I told him because of his attitude and countenance changing, he was to give his notice to the manager that day, because he would be quitting. A sixteen year old young man did not want to do this, but out of obedience and respect for us, he would. About a month later, Stan and I went to the movie theatre. While we were in the movie, the manager came and gave us a letter to look at. The letter was written to convince us to let Shawn come back to work there. He said, "Shawn was a great influence on all the employees and I need his positive attitude around them. Please would you reconsider and let me hire Shawn back?" We were shocked at the amount of effort this manager took to seek us out and try to convince us to let Shawn come back. Needless to say, we didn't. But what a testimony of how we should influence those around us. We need to show the love of Jesus no matter where we are.

Another job Shawn had was at a Christian bookstore. Again, we got letter after letter from managers, letting us know what a good influence Shawn was and how he was always full of joy. Never in all my years of life have I had people rave about my services and how good of a job I did, like Shawn has. Shawn has been a great encourager to all who are around him— you can just see the joy of the Lord.

Lord, let us all become so full of your joy that we radiate

it from us in everything we do! Help us to become *The Perfect Touch*, full of joy!

Shawn has become one of the greatest servants of the Lord I have ever seen. He is a young man, full of energy and life, a perfect specimen of an Evangelist. One who gets you yelling, "Yea! I will! You bet I'll do that." He gets you fired up. Shawn made a decision at a very young age to serve the Lord and to be His servant to all. Because of his obedience, Shawn has become one of the greatest preachers I have ever seen or heard. It's really incredible when you are so caught up in what the preacher is saying; he is causing you to change areas in your life that need changing; and then, all of a sudden you look at him different. He is my son, my child. Wow, what a strange feeling! Thanks to Shawn's hearing and obeying the Lord, he is able to use *The Perfect Touch* of the Lord to touch many people's lives.

The Lord spoke to Shawn during the middle of the night not long ago. Jesus was convicting Shawn of some areas in his life that needed correction. During the night, Shawn kept seeing the words, **"NEVER AGAIN"**. Jesus loves him so much, that everywhere in the dream Shawn looked, he saw those words. Jesus loves us that much, also. He will chasten the ones He loves. He wants total repentance and a total turning of your heart towards Him. Shawn wrote a letter to God. The following is that letter. Let it minister to you and I pray that there will be **"NEVER AGAIN"** in your life.

Dear Savior, My Love, My Beautiful King:

Words cannot express my sorrow for the pain I've caused You. Even before I entered in sin, I knew You would forgive. Maybe that is why I fell so easily. I made a mockery of Your incredible grace and continued to fall before Your own eyes. I only had good intentions to change. I brag about You and tell everyone I love you, but behind closed doors, I deny Your beautiful face, the very one that stared at me in moments of complete intimacy.

I know I've said this before, and I pray You hear me, even this time, as You have every time before. I am sorry, I don't want to hurt You. I miss Your arms around me, I miss Your kisses upon my head and heart. Please forgive me. I say I am black, but you say I am lovely (**Song of Solomon 1:5**). I don't understand this, but I am so grateful.

Jesus, tonight, I'm making a vow - a covenant to You. More than a statement, more than a good intention, even more than an admittance of guilt, but a vow to never hurt You in this manner again. **Never Again.** Engrave it in every part of my heart, life, soul and mind. Any part of me that deals with making a decision, engrave the words - **Never Again** - so I am constantly reminded.

This pain is way beyond me. If only the world, or even a lot of my Christian brothers and sisters knew your heart. Surely they would find all the answers, and happiness in You. Your love is sweeter than wine, more precious and beautiful than anything this world has to offer. O God, overwhelm me with your grace and forgiveness. Never again will I hurt you like this. I love You. -Shawn

Finally, I want to share *The Perfect Touch,* I have received from my daughter, Leslie Ann. I always desired a daughter, and as a fool, prayed for one just like me. Oh man! That is exactly what we got—only a stronger personality and more independent. I'm not sure if God used His *Perfect Touch* or not. Just kidding! She is an awesome young woman of the Lord. She has so many talents, gifts and goals in life, and I am sure she will use every one of them in the Lord's Kingdom.

When she was born, my dad sent me a dozen pink roses. On the card it read, "Daddy's hands picked these." I knew that the Lord had made this little one special for Him from that very first day. I knew my heavenly Father picked this one out. Even at a young age, Leslie Ann has a lot of wisdom and discernment. She knows who people are when she first meets them. She sees right to their heart. She does have *The Perfect Touch* from God, because people become aware when Leslie Ann is in a room. She makes an effect on people's lives. There is something that God has placed in her to be noticed, and an ability to capture your heart. Leslie Ann does dance interpretation of the Lord's praise and worship, and she sings beautifully. We never knew this talent was even there until a few years ago.

One day I noticed a tape had appeared on my desk. That particular tape had been missing for about ten years, when all of a sudden, it just showed up. Being so excited, I ran to the tape player and called out for Leslie Ann to come and hear this song. This was a song that I had asked the Lord, ten years prior, to give me the dance interpretation for. At that time He spoke to me and said, "No, I want you to sing this song for me."

I thought, "Yeah right! I can't sing, I heard the Lord wrong on this one."

Finally, Leslie Ann came into the room and listened to the song for a few moments. I will never forget what she did next. She turned around to me, and out of her mouth came these words. She said, "Mom, this song is not for me, it is for you. You are suppose to sing it."

I immediately thought, "Oh no! I know she is right." She had heard the perfect Word of the Lord. I began asking her to help me get it prepared, and in the meantime, kept trying to get her to sing the song, but to no avail. I was suppose to sing it.

The Lord spoke to me, and said, "If you will humble yourself before me, I will anoint your voice and each time you do a song unto me, I will make it stronger and more anointed."

Sometimes we think the Lord asks us to do the impossible. In my heart of heart, I desired to praise and worship the Lord with my whole being. This was one more step in that direction.

Leslie Ann and I worked on the song for about a week. Knowing the Sunday morning worship time was going to be my debut, we had planned to go to the church on Saturday afternoon, when no one was there, so I could practice with the microphone. Yes! That was what we were going to do; however, there was just one problem. Early that Saturday morning, all of a sudden it occurred to me, I didn't know how to turn on the sound equipment. I was going to have to tell my husband. Needing his help, I went to Stan and said, "I have something important to tell you." I kept crying and crying to my husband. Like most husbands, he thought I had done something terribly wrong and spent too much money. (Men, you think you have figured us women out. I don't know why you think that, because we can't even figure ourselves out.) Finally, I spit it out about the song God wanted me to sing on Sunday. My husband was so wonderful—and so relieved and happy that I didn't spend any money on an expensive outfit, or buy another dog! I stepped out in faith because of my daughter. She is a real encourager and can get you to do things you wouldn't normally do. I have been so blessed by that experience. Because my daughter heard from the Lord and spoke those words, I received *The Perfect Touch* from God.

Leslie Ann has many talents and gifts from her heavenly father. But, one of the most dynamic gifts comes from what the world would call, great charisma and great stage presence. I know this is a gift from God, because from the time Leslie Ann could talk, she would talk about being on stage in front of people. She wanted to have people notice her. This was not in a bad or egotistical way, just in a way that she could relate to people. She wanted to get them involved in what she was doing. You can train a voice, be talented with a musical instrument, be a great dancer, but stage presence is inborn. It is a gift from the most high King. Leslie Ann has that gift from God. She will make her goal! God has given her a determination that is more prominent in her than any adult I have ever met. Remember that name—Leslie Ann. She will be used for the Lord in a great big way!

Wouldn't it be nice to receive *The Perfect Touch* from the Lord at a very young age, and know exactly what your call is in life? Wouldn't it be nice to be determined in the Lord, to fulfill the dream He has for you? Leslie Ann has shared these words, "I have never known what it is like to not be saved. I have known Jesus all my life, and I can't remember not knowing Him as my Lord and Savior." My prayer for Leslie Ann is that she will someday be a beautiful old lady and still be able to say those same words. I pray she never steers away. She will always know Jesus as her King, Master, Lord and Savior.

In our lives we can learn to recognize *The Perfect Touch* from the Lord through our family members. Just think about it for a while. Our moms and dads, sisters and brothers, our in-laws have all had an impact on our lives. Try and remember an encouraging word that came out of their mouths. A sacrifice they made for you, a helping hand or just a hug.

I came from a great family of four sisters and two brothers, and had wonderful parents. However, like so many homes these days, my parents were divorced when we were young.

Through the hard times that all of us go through growing up, I have realized so much of how we act and respond when we get older, has to do with a decision we made in the past. I have one brother, Marty, who made a decision that he would stay peaceful. Marty definitely has become the peacemaker of the family. He is the glue that holds us all together. The main reason that Marty can be this way is that he is a Christian with a strong belief in the Lord, and is a true servant to all who are around him. We can count on him and we know we are going to get an encouraging word when we call him. He is not stingy on giving *The Perfect Touch* from our Lord. He will always strive to reach out and touch us with love, compassion and peace.

We can give *The Perfect Touch* to our loved ones also. Sometimes just making that effort to say I love you, or just a hug is all it takes. Some of you are thinking right now, "Well, I didn't have a great life growing up. There was not any love in our home." It is never too late to be the first to start. You be that encourager, the one to say I love you, the one to give a hug or a word of praise. It is never too late. Too many times we wait until someone else makes the first move. God is waiting for us to make the first move. When you have done all—stand. In other words, when **you** have done all. Reach out and touch someone you love and care for. Make the first and last move. Mountains will be removed. You wait and see!

Remember, "Never Again", could change things around for *The Perfect Touch.*

The Perfect Touch

Chapter 10

Turn On the Light

*H*ave you ever received that perfect present from a friend? I have, and receiving *The Perfect Touch* from friends is so special. Fortunately, I have so many instances to share. You know when you associate yourself with the right people, you and everything turns out right. The Scriptures say that we are not to fellowship with others who are not of the same belief we are.

1 Corinthians 10:20 *But I say, that the things which the Gentiles sacrifice, they sacrifice to devils, and not to God: and I would not that ye should have fellowship with devils.*

2 Corinthians 6:14 *Be ye not unequally yoked together with unbelievers: for what fellowship hath righteousness with unrighteousness? and what communion hath light with darkness?*

Ephesians 5:11 *And have no fellowship with the unfruitful works of darkness, but rather reprove them.*

Notice, the Lord asks us a question, what communion hath light with darkness? We are not to associate with darkness.

1 John 1:6-7 *If we say that we have fellowship with him, and walk in darkness, we lie, and do not the truth: But if we walk in the light, as he is in the light, we have fellowship one with another, and the blood of Jesus Christ his Son cleanseth us from all sin.*

89

The Perfect Touch

When God answers a prayer, and the prayer is revealed through a friend right before our eyes, you know that you have received *The Perfect Touch* from a special friend.

Proverbs 18:24 ***A man that hath friends must shew himself friendly: and there is a friend that sticketh closer than a brother.***

Proverbs 27:10 ***Thine own friend, and thy father's friend, forsake not; neither go into thy brother's house in the day of thy calamity: for better is a neighbour that is near than a brother far off.***

The Johnson family has a special family who has been there for us so many times. I will never forget this family and how they heard from the Lord and responded with *The Perfect Touch* for us one day. It was early in our walk, as full-time in the ministry, and Stan had just quit his good paying secular job to do what the Lord was directing us to do. Here it was, the day before Thanksgiving and we had no groceries. I had already done all the creative cooking possible. You know, throw a can of this in the pot and another can of that stuff, and might as well throw in this box of goodies, too. I was starting to get a little concerned—all right, a lot concerned—because friends and family were invited to come over for Thanksgiving Dinner. Going up to Stan, I asked him, "Do you have any money stashed anywhere?"

Unfortunately, the answer Stan gave me was, "No."

Now, I was really getting discouraged and thought, "You know, I have never had Thanksgiving dinner without a turkey. I guess we could have peanut butter sandwiches, but it would have to be without the jelly."

Stan took my hands in his and raised them up to the Lord. He said, "Lord, you say in your Word, that you will provide. You will hold up our hands. We ask that you will do a miracle and provide us with Thanksgiving dinner, in Jesus

Name!" Simple, yet nothing is more powerful than the name of Jesus. A few hours later, *The Perfect Touch*, from that very special friend, Jo and her children, showed up at our door with arms full of groceries.

She said, "Leslie, I was at the grocery store and all of a sudden, I was impressed to get all the trimmings for you for Thanksgiving dinner." She said, "Move over, I'm going to prepare it for you and cook the dinner for you." God kept multiplying the food. I'm telling you, we had so much food, enough for several days. "Praise you Jesus!"

The Lord wants to use each one of us, to do something special for the friends He has given us. If we will just listen to our King, He will prompt us by putting them on our heart, but it is up to us to pray and see if there is something special the Lord would like for us to do. It might be groceries. It might be providing them dinner. It might be just a call to say I was thinking about you. It might be mowing a lawn or giving them money. Be obedient to what the Lord lays on your heart for a friend. Do not ignore that prompting. They are probably praying for someone to hear and obey the voice of the Lord. "Lord, let us become *The Perfect Touch*, that special servant to someone."

The Lord has blessed me with people all my life who have been there for me. The people I remember the most though, are the ones since I have been saved and filled with the Baptism of the Holy Spirit. Just prior to this moment in my life, we had started a block Bible study in our home. There were several Christians on the block and we desired to get a Bible study going. We decided to have it every Friday night. The first Friday we had the Bible study, two ladies from our neighborhood came. As these two ladies walked in, I felt something special on them and around them. There was definitely something different about them. I watched them closely that night and observed everything they did and said. At the end of the meeting, I cornered these two ladies and inquired, "There is something special you both have from Jesus and I want it. How do I get what you have?"

One of them handed me a booklet by Kenneth Hagin, *The Bible Way to Receive the Baptism of the Holy Spirit*. The Lord had already prepared her to bring the booklet that evening. She said, "Read this and if you have any questions, you can call one of us. Next week we will talk with you about this."

After they left, my thought was, "Next week?" You see, they didn't know me very well. There was no way I was going to wait a week to receive a gift from God. I couldn't wait. I made a plan, and thought, "I will wait until Monday night. Stan won't be coming home until late from work, and I will get the children to bed as early as possible. Then the Lord and I are going to have a talk. Yea! That's what I am going to do."

Monday night came, and to my surprise the children went to bed early very easily that evening. I looked at the clock and thought, "Okay, I have two hours before Stan will be home." I took the booklet and sat in the middle of the living room floor and began to read this small little book. I remember thinking, "Okay, it isn't very many pages. I can read through this and get what those other ladies have real quick." I read that booklet as quickly as I could. At the end, it gave several steps to go through to receive the Baptism of the Holy Spirit. I went through those steps and wow, all of a sudden, a new language was coming from my mouth. I was so excited, even though I really had no concept of what really happened to me, I kept on and on speaking this new language. It felt great! It felt wonderful! It felt like I had received something from God. I went to bed so excited! It was getting late, but there was no way I could go to sleep, so I got my Bible. Even though it was King James, I could read and understand what the scriptures were saying. Never before had the Word of the Lord made so much sense. It was awesome!

I heard the garage door opening and realized that Stan was about to come in. I thought, "I can't be reading the Bible when he comes in, because he will really think something is up." All of a sudden, I had a thought of panic. "Oh, No! Stan is not going to like this. I speak in tongues! He might think it is from the devil. I'll just pray. Maybe he won't find out!"

The next day I was consumed with the Word of God. It was like I had never read a word in the Bible before. It came alive. It was real. It was easier to understand. It was great! I often joke that my Bible was the first Rainbow Bible, because you should see all the different shades of highlights. Everything that came alive to me was highlighted. Now, almost all of the New Testament is in different colors.

Just when I thought things were safe, the next evening when Stan came home, we met in the hall. As we were passing by each other, he turned me around and he said to me, "Okay, what is it?"

I'm thinking, "Oh no! Surely he didn't figure it out." I know he didn't see the booklet because I had it with me the whole time. I said to Stan with a gulp, "What is it?"

Stan said, "You are different."

I thought, "Oh man, this is it." I wasn't going to be able to keep it a secret, no matter how hard I tried. As I began telling Stan what happened, I spoke to him so fast it was like a blur to him. Talking 90 miles an hour, I said, "I read this booklet, *The Bible Way to Receive the Baptism of the Holy Spirit*, so I asked for it, I received it, and I speak in tongues. Here, you read it and you can receive the gift also!" Hoping to get away quickly, after saying all of those words, I started to walk off.

Stan asked, "What?" So, I repeated it even faster the second time. Stan's reaction the second time around was just as I thought. He said, "No, no. I'm not reading a booklet. If it is in the Bible, I will see it and then I will believe it."

After a few weeks of Stan observing such a difference in me, he began to study all the verses in the Bible that had Holy Spirit and Holy Ghost in the Word. My new friends in the neighborhood and myself began to pray for him to see the truth and desire this wonderful gift from God.

After several weeks of studying, Stan came to me one evening and said, "I believe the Baptism of the Holy Spirit is from God. I see there is a Baptism of water and of the Holy Ghost. I want to receive this gift from Jesus. Call the other ladies and all of you pray for me to receive. The Bible says they laid hands on them and they received the gifts of the Holy Spirit. I'm going to do this the Bible way." Hallelujah! Our prayers were answered and Stan received *The Perfect Touch* from the Lord that evening.

Acts 8:17 *Then laid they their hands on them, and they received the Holy Ghost.*

Our Lord is no respecter of persons. He will give the gift to all who desire and ask. We must come with a clean heart and repent of all occultic activities in our lives. Cover these sins in the Blood of Jesus and remit the sins. He will inhabit the clean vessels. I have heard from people over the years that their life wasn't changed when they received the Baptism of the Holy Spirit. Some say they don't have to speak in tongues, but they know they received the baptism. Let me ask you a question. If the lesser of the gifts is speaking in tongues and we get all the gifts when we receive the baptism, then why would Jesus not give you the gift of tongues? This is the evidence that you received the gift of the Baptism of the Holy Spirit. Too many times we want to be in control. We need to let loose and let God be in charge of our lives. We make too much of a mess of things when we control our lives—especially you men, because of the nature God has put in you. Generally you will find it harder to let the Holy Spirit take over your life. You men want to conquer. Once a man realizes that he truly wants God to be in control, then the Baptism of the Holy Spirit with the gift of tongues comes forth.

My life has never been the same upon receiving the Baptism of the Holy Spirit. I am much bolder and on fire for my Jesus. There was such a difference for the better in my life, and it can be for you also. Receive *The Perfect Touch.*

Once you receive this baptism, there must be a change that takes place in your life. The Baptism of the Holy Spirit is for boldness, power and witnessing. If you have asked for the

Baptism of the Holy Spirit and even if you speak in another tongue, but you say there was no change in your life, I would question and challenge whether you really got the Baptism of the Holy Ghost. From those whom I know personally, who truly received the gift from God, they were changed. The devil has filtered into our churches over the years, and has tried to convince many that the gifts of the Holy Spirit and speaking in tongues were for the Apostles—only for the people back then. Oh, really! Then what do you do with these scriptures?

Hebrews 13:8 *Jesus Christ the same yesterday, and to day, and for ever.*

Acts 19:4 *Then said Paul, John verily baptized with the baptism of repentance, saying unto the people, that they should believe on him which should come after him, that is, on Christ Jesus.*

Mark 16:17-18 *And these signs shall follow them that believe; In my name shall they cast out devils; they shall speak with new tongues; They shall take up serpents; and if they drink any deadly thing, it shall not hurt them; they shall lay hands on the sick, and they shall recover.*

Acts 2:4 *And they were all filled with the Holy Ghost, and began to speak with other tongues, as the Spirit gave them utterance.*

1 Corinthians 14:39 *Wherefore, brethren, covet to prophesy, and forbid not to speak with tongues.*

When we yield to the Holy Spirit we can have greater communication with our Lord. Isn't that what we all want? Do you want to be freer and filled with the joy of the Lord? As we submit our life, as we pray in tongues building our faith, as we seek to hear and do the will of God in our life, we are much happier people. We are to have understanding of the will of

God in our life. Reach out to that next level if you have never experienced the gifts of the Holy Ghost. Our Lord is ready and willing to give to all who ask. Come with a clean heart, a clean conscience, and repent of all ungodly sins and soul ties. Receive *The Perfect Touch* from Jesus and be baptized with His Holy Spirit!

Jude 1:20 *But ye, beloved, building up yourselves on your most holy faith, praying in the Holy Ghost,*

John 7:17 *If any man will do his will, he shall know of the doctrine, whether it be of God, or whether I speak of myself.*

John 9:31 *Now we know that God heareth not sinners: but if any man be a worshipper of God, and doeth his will, him he heareth.*

John 10:5 *And a stranger will they not follow, but will flee from him: for they know not the voice of strangers.*

Colossians 1:9 *For this cause we also, since the day we heard it, do not cease to pray for you, and to desire that ye might be filled with the knowledge of his will in all wisdom and spiritual understanding;*

Just ask and you can receive the gifts with *The Perfect Touch.*

Chapter 11

Pack Your Bags Light

Sometimes we decide to be isolated from family and friends, or the world in general. Being isolated is a choice we make. I might add, it is usually a selfish act. God doesn't want us to be unsocial, self-centered or isolated. The Word of the Lord says that we are to fellowship with each other.

Acts 2:42 *And they continued stedfastly in the apostles' doctrine and fellowship, and in breaking of bread, and in prayers.*

When people become isolated, many times a feeling of 'nobody loves me' attitude is apparent. This type of person complains about not having any friends; that nobody likes them; they complain that they are just too shy, and many times the focus becomes on how terrible other people treated them. I know that sometimes evil things happen to people; but the point is all of us could complain about something in our childhood, past marriage, or some evil thing that has happened to us. What the Lord would want us to do is give Him our burdens. The more we cling to things from the past and not go forward, the more the enemy has control of our lives. If you are carrying all that excess baggage, it will get really heavy. It is much better to carry the joy of the Lord and release those burdens to Him. The more you rehearse the past, the more you want it to be bandaged up. All of a sudden the bandage is so big and bulky that all of your focus is on that incident. We are to say to that mountain, be removed. I like to hang around someone positive with the joy of the Lord, don't you? There are times we need to help each other out of the pit we have fallen into; however, it starts with you making a decision, declaring a choice to get the joy of the Lord and be happy.

I am blessed to say that I have some great, wonderful friends. They make me happy, they make me laugh, we talk of things the Lord is doing in our lives, and if needed, some of the cares we have. My dad always told me a saying that I am sure many of you have heard before, "You can't hang around with the wrong type of people and expect to turn out right." My children have heard this saying often enough, but I truly believe it. I have often given my children an example of how they should always remember this important saying. My explanation to them is: Let's say that you are on top of a pool table, and you are looking down at a friend telling him all about Jesus. You take your friend's hand and try to pull him up on the pool table with you. Now the question is; while trying to pull your friend up, is your friend going to pull you down? Who do you think is going to win? The one pulling the other one up onto the pool table or the one pulling you down? Of course, the answer is the one pulling you down. We must not be unequally yoked.

Our Lord and Savior has given us so many choices to make in our lives and we mess up all the time. Even though He could stop terrible things from happening in our lives, we would then lose our free will. Not one of us wants to do that. So many things in life are from choices we make, whether they be good or bad. I have a young friend in the Lord coming to our church. He is newly saved and Baptized in the Holy Spirit. He is so hungry to be around Christians. All of his worldly, drug and drinking friends have left him. "Praise the Lord!" He realizes that he can't hang around with them, or as he says, "kick it with 'em". He is wanting to fellowship with my children and others in the church and be there every time the doors are open. He gave a testimony in the church on how if you continue to hang around with the people following Satan, then no matter how strong you think you are in Christ, they will continue to work on you until you fall again. He is so right. We need to know and see the fruit of the Spirit in the people we fellowship with. This young man could become isolated, but how is he going to stay accountable and get stronger? We must choose Godly Christians to hang around and to not isolate ourselves. Receiving loving correction and guidance from Godly counsel is wisdom.

Proverbs 8:14-15 *Counsel is mine, and sound wisdom: I am understanding; I have strength. By me kings reign, and princes decree justice.*

Proverbs 1:5-19 *A wise man will hear, and will increase learning; and a man of understanding shall attain unto wise counsels: To understand a proverb, and the interpretation; the words of the wise, and their dark sayings. The fear of the LORD is the beginning of knowledge: but fools despise wisdom and instruction. My son, hear the instruction of thy father, and forsake not the law of thy mother: For they shall be an ornament of grace unto thy head, and chains about thy neck. My son, if sinners entice thee, consent thou not. If they say, Come with us, let us lay wait for blood, let us lurk privily for the innocent without cause: Let us swallow them up alive as the grave; and whole, as those that go down into the pit: We shall find all precious substance, we shall fill our houses with spoil: Cast in thy lot among us; let us all have one purse: My son, walk not thou in the way with them; refrain thy foot from their path: For their feet run to evil, and make haste to shed blood. Surely in vain the net is spread in the sight of any bird. And they lay wait for their own blood; they lurk privily for their own lives. So are the ways of every one that is greedy of gain; which taketh away the life of the owners thereof.*

Find a Godly Christian friend. Don't wait until they find you. You make the choice. Go, look and you will find, then you can disperse *The Perfect Touch* to someone else.

Friends come in all shapes, forms, and personalities. Some friends God actually puts in our path. The friends we have at our business were truly brought there from the Lord Himself. He placed everyone of them there. Sharon, one of the ladies who works for us, said, "I had absolutely no intention in working for Stan and you." She told us that Joyce, another wonderful woman of God who works for us, convinced her to come and see about a possible position. Sharon said, "I was just going to come and talk to you two to make her happy." Well, God had other intentions, she found herself saying yes to a position working for us. She has told us she went walking out shaking her head, and saying, "I can't believe I just said yes. I couldn't say no."

All I've got to say is, "HALLELUJAH! PRAISE THE LORD!" You see, I just received *The Perfect Touch* from the Lord, because the position she was taking was mine. Yea! God was answering my prayer and He also gave me a good friend. I often tell her, you are my favorite person in the whole world. You are my best friend. Truly, she is a gift from God.

Friends help keep us in balance. They can say things to keep us on the right path, where maybe a spouse or someone else cannot. Also, they can be encouragers to our spouse and keep them on the right track. I've had several friends over the years who were able to call up Stan or myself and ever so gently get us on the right track when either one of us were out of balance with each other. Friends learn to read our faces, stress marks, (not stretch marks! ha ha) and body language sometimes much faster and easier than our spouse. I have a couple of friends who we can take turns to just dump—rarely, I might add. Sometimes to keep from getting further frustrated, we have to dump. You know what this is women. We don't want anything fixed, we just want to dump. We've earned the right, we've earned the frustration, we've earned the cry and we've earned being mad. We just want someone to listen to us while we pour it all out to them, and not just one time through I might add. These are good friends to have because after you are done, they won't try to fix the situation, they will just nicely get us back on the right track and get us back in balance. Sometimes you know that was *The Perfect Touch* of God.

As Christians, we need to learn to not hold on to offenses. Holding on to offenses only continues to hurt us in our walk with the Lord. We need to learn to get over trespasses against us quickly. The Word of the Lord says we are not to go to bed with anger on our heart. If we hold on to these trespasses, guess what? We can become gossipers. Yes men, I am speaking to you also. Men tend to think if they are talking about someone at their job or business, then that is not gossiping—talking about someone, telling others about a problem, etc. Now that is not gossiping, right? Get the point.

Ephesians 4:31 *Let all bitterness, and wrath, and anger, and clamour, and evil speaking, be put away from you, with all malice:*

Ephesians 4:26 *Be ye angry, and sin not: let not the sun go down upon your wrath:*

Release those people right now, if you hold a grudge against someone. Do not hold yourself or others in bondage.

A vision that was given to my friend, Joyce, shows just where we are if we don't let go of offenses. As Christian brothers and sisters, we need to finally unite. This is what she said, "I saw tired and haggard soldiers emerging from a forest. They were walking slowly—spread apart one or two at a time. There were also two soldiers carrying a stretcher, with a badly wounded soldier on it. In one way or another everyone was wounded. Some had white bandages wrapped around their head, or bandages around the upper arm or upper thigh. Some were walking with crutches, others just limping—none were spared from having a visible wound. Then I noticed, not one of them had a shield—they were all trying to fight their own battles! The Lord said, "Where's your faith? Where are your shields? Grow up! Unite! Stop thinking and pitying yourselves! You MUST believe and receive your own healing—emotional and physical—before going into battle, and NEVER, no **NEVER**, take your eyes off of Me (Jesus). You must unite! You are only as strong as your weakest soldier. Kneel—put your shields together—the fiery darts will bounce off. Immerse yourselves in the WORD. I will destroy your enemies—keep your eyes focused on Me!

"Then I saw a vision of hundreds of soldiers, standing close together with big shields. They all kneeled on one knee (planting themselves firm), and locked all their shields together so no dart or stone could fall in between them. The enemy shot hundreds of their fiery darts upon the shields. They all bounced off like rubber bouncing balls—not one dart penetrated through or between the shields!"

The most important thing is to notice that they were locking all of their shields together, so no dart or stone could fall in between them. They were united. There is more power when we unite, instead of fighting the battle alone. The word unite means to put or bring together so as to make one; combine or joining into a whole. To bring together in common cause, interest, opinion. Join in action, through fellowship, agreement, to cause to adhere. This is what the Lord wants for us, to become united. Jesus is our common cause!

Remember, let your best friend, Jesus, give you *The Perfect Touch.*

Chapter 12

Feathers, Bricks, Noodles & Butter

Receiving freedom is a wonderful touch from the Lord. We can walk in the joy of the Lord at all times. How do we do this? We are to praise the Lord in all things. Once you become free from all bondages, when you receive *The Perfect Touch* from the Holy Spirit, it is an awesome experience. When the power of God hits you, you know He is ministering to you. Because of His power, a person may go slain in the Spirit or fall down—similar to passing out—when someone lays their hands on you and prays.

Once I had a woman come to me and say she was scared for me to pray for her because she did not want to go slain in the Spirit. I said to her, "I have no control over what the Lord chooses to do." There have been times when I asked the Lord, "Please if you would, don't have this person go slain in the Spirit." I do this for a specific reason at the time, but it is the Lord's ultimate choice, not mine. I asked her, "Do you want me to pray for you or not?"

She said, "I do, but I am scared."

I told her, "The first thing we need to do is get rid of that spirit of fear on you!" Before I even laid hands on her, we prayed against that spirit. Then she asked what it felt like when someone went slain in the Spirit. I told her that I could only speak from my experience and from what others say. It varies at different times. There have been times when I was totally unaware of what was going on around me, yet other times I could see and hear what was going on around me, but I could not get up. There have been instances where I was so drunk in the Spirit, that I could not get up, and other occasions when I have just laid there and laughed. There have been times I have been on the floor for long periods of time, and other times not long at all. It all depends on what the touch of the Lord wants to do. It is not up to me. I do know that each and every time the Lord was ministering to me. In most instances it was very evident, and at other times, I was not real sure what the Lord was ministering to my Spirit. There is one thing I do know, the Holy Spirit is real and He will accomplish what He wants. We make the choice whether to be ministered to by the Holy Spirit or not. At that point, I asked the lady if she truly wanted to be ministered to by the Lord. Once the fear left her, she made a decision and I prayed for her. The Lord had her go slain in the Spirit, and I mean slain in the Spirit for quite a long time. That whole weekend you could see her countenance changing. She was receiving such freedom and the joy of the Lord. Our Lord is so awesome! He will meet us right where we are, and then take us a step further, if we will just yield to His Holy Spirit.

Receiving the anointing from the Lord for people to go slain in the Spirit is caught. First, you must submit to the Holy Spirit, whether anyone is laying hands on you or not. I for one, am a person who says, "Lord, if it is from you and I can have it, then whatever it is I want it!" I'm the type who doesn't even like to wait to open presents. I want the present as soon as I see it, as a matter of fact, if the opportunity exist (I usually make one) then I will peek. That is what I feel like with the Lord. I don't just want His anointing, nor just a double portion anointing, I want more. I want as much as the Lord knows I can handle.

When the power of God hits you, you might wonder at first, did I make myself go down, or did the person praying for me push me down? No, the Lord is ministering to you. The Lord ministers differently with each person, as well as different times.

One Sunday morning, while praying for my husband, I knew when he came up for me to pray for him that the Lord was going to touch him mightily. Stan, the man with control and so debonair, had in the past resisted going slain in the Spirit. He had many questions concerning this phenomenon; however, this day would be different because Stan desired all that God had for him. As Stan came up for prayer, my hands did not even touch him, when pow, Stan went down. He went down hard—like a brick! He said it was a force so strong that it knocked him down. As he was going down, he yelled out loud, "umph" and fell down in a sitting position and then laid back. He started laughing in the Spirit and rejoicing, as he was saying, "So this is what it is like to be slain in the Spirit." It was so awesome to see *The Perfect Touch* of the Holy Spirit get a hold of Stan that morning. Stan said to me, "Where did you place your hands on me?"

I explained, "I was going to place them on each side of your cheeks, but I didn't get the chance."

He said, "It felt like a powerful push in my stomach and a powerful knock on my forehead, and a powerful force pushed me down." I told him my hands never even touch his forehead. Now he has caught the anointing and many people he prays for go slain in the Spirit.

Another time a lady came up for prayer and each time I would lay my hands on her to pray she would jump back. I would look at her and she kept saying to me, "Are you pushing me?" I assured her I wasn't pushing her. She said, "Every time you touch me, I feel like you are pushing me real hard."

I said, "Look, I will just put my finger up to you and I will barely touch you." As I did this, I said, "By the power of the Holy Spirit" and wow, the Spirit of the Lord knocked her flat down on the ground.

Dan, a brother in the Lord praying with me for people, said "Wow, I guess God wanted to do something powerful in her."

She got up later and said, "Man, it felt like you pushed me real hard."

Dan said, "Lady, if you don't know who did that powerful thing for you, your crazy. Leslie barely even touched you, I was standing here with her watching."

When you are free to receive what the Holy Spirit wants, the impartation from the person praying for you is transferred. The anointing, for the most part, is caught. From experience I have noticed there are different types of anointing and how people respond when going slain in the Spirit. There are those people who receive the anointing very easily. They are so hungry and thirsty for what God wants, they receive very willingly, and many with a smile on their face. They fall back into the presence of the Lord with such a peace over them.

Then there are the ones who seem to receive a real power push down, so they go floating. It is my observation that most of the time when this happens, the Lord is ministering healing to their body. Sometimes, when there is such a powerful hit from the Lord, the body moves around like it is being adjusted. I witnessed a lady having her face and jaw completely realigned. She came up for prayer and said that because of a disease she had, her face was becoming disfigured and it caused much pain in her jaw. Her jaw was misplaced to one side of her face. When I laid hands on her, the power hit this little lady and down she went. Her face began to move and her body was realigned. She laid there a good long while. The Lord ministered to that precious woman and healed her body that evening. She came up to me the next day, and said, "Look at me, I look totally different. God has put my face back on straight." She was so beautiful.

One time while praying for this gentleman, who was 6'7" tall, (I am only 5 foot tall, and I barely came to his waist.) I asked the Lord, "Now Lord, how am I to reach this man's cheeks, much less his forehead?" I know, I'll get a chair. So that's what I did.

As I laid my hands on this man, I got a Word from the Lord for him. He saw himself very small in the work of the Lord. The Lord said, "I want you to fill those big shoes I have given you for the work of the ministry." He was a big man with a big compassionate heart.

As I continued to speak the Word of the Lord to him, this big man began to weep. I asked the Lord, "What do you want me to do now?"

The Lord said, "I am going to minister to him now." And with that, this huge man went floating down in the Spirit.

He later came to me and said, "If dynamite comes in small packages and if the Spirit of the Lord is in this lady, then I know I will receive the anointing God has for me. You are so small compared to me and that there would be no way you could knock me down, so I knew if I went slain in the Spirit, then it would have to be God." This man just floated down like a feather. It was so cool!

Other times when people get prayed for and go slain in the Spirit, they just sit down. Now these type of people make it very difficult for the catchers, if there are any. Again, like Stan, he just sat down hard and then laid back. I have noticed that these people usually get the laughter of the Lord. I guess the Lord wants to give them an extra dose of joy, and usually they are needing that very thing. These types remind me of a little toddler falling down and going, boom! Haven't you seen a toddler fall on their behind and begin to laugh?

The most difficult people going slain in the Spirit, at least for the catchers, are you wet noodle types. You stand there like a strong straight spaghetti noodle and then when hands are laid on you, you just go limp like a wet spaghetti noodle. It is so funny to me to watch the catchers with these people. Catchers are not necessary, because when it is God, you don't get hurt. It is just a courtesy to have a catcher.

At one of our Crusades, a gentleman who was catching people as I prayed for them, waited until the very end and then asked me to pray for him. I motioned to Stephen, our praise and worship leader, to stand behind this man while I prayed for him. Now, Stephen is huge, I call him my bodyguard. He is 6'3" and weighs about 300 pounds. I thought for sure with Stephen catching this other man—no problem. I tease Stephen, because after praying for this man, he went down like a wet noodle and slid right between Stephen's legs. It was one of the funniest things I have seen happen. The noodles seem to get an extra anointing.

So far, we have the feathers, the bricks, and the noodles, and we can't forget those like me—the melted butter type. They call me the meltdown queen. I go down so fast that no one can catch me. Recently there were three men behind me ready to catch me. Before they knew what happened, I was down for the count. It was during that time I received visions, direction, and a stronger anointing.

Also, let's not forget the falling forward people. This power from the Holy Spirit is challenging for me, because the catchers are behind you and I am in front of you. So guess who gets to catch you? Just recently in one of the meetings, I had at least four people go forward. Someone once told me that if a person goes forward, it is because of demonic activity in their life. If that were true, then probably almost everyone would go forward. The devil is out to kill, steal and destroy our lives. I don't worry about which way, or how, or even whether a person will go slain in the Spirit. This is totally up to Jesus what He wants to do. I am just being a willing vessel for Him to work through.

When I think of *The Perfect Touch*, it often reminds me about the woman who touched the hem of His garment and she was healed. If we could just grab hold of that kind of faith. We just need to reach out and touch His hem. The Bible gives us examples of how *The Perfect Touch* of Jesus was important.

Mark 5:27 *When she had heard of Jesus, came in the press behind, and touched his garment.*

In Mark 6:5, Jesus laid his hands upon the sick and they were healed. In Luke 22:51, Jesus touched his ear and he was healed. I have personally received *The Perfect Touch* from the Lord in healing my ears. **(Lord, I pray as those who read this chapter, that you will supernaturally heal them in whatever their need is. Jesus, I pray compassion on each person and I thank you in advance for divine healing in Jesus' name.)**

I know that if Jesus will do it for me, He will do it for you. Just have faith. Remember Hebrews 11:1, that faith is a substance. It is something you can grab hold of.

We were on our way to a Crusade that we were conducting, and the enemy was fighting us hard. Many of the leaders were coming down sick. I had a terrible ear ache, and I have not had an ear infection since I was four years old. Finally I had to go to the doctor because of the dizziness and excruciating pain. The doctor gave me some eardrops and said that in a couple of days my ear would be better. In the next couple of days my hearing became so impaired out of my right ear, that it was hard to hear. By Monday it was so clogged and painful, I went to see another doctor. This doctor said that actually both ears were clogged and she wanted to put fluid in my ear and then drain it to unclog the ear canal. She said, "Lets start with the good ear, your left one, and do it first." When the nurse began the procedure, all of a sudden somehow she burst my eardrum by mistake. I felt like I was going to pass out from so much pain. Obviously the doctor and nurse felt very bad—she gave me prescriptions and sent me home.

The next day I was to fly to Portland, Oregon. This would be a long day, plus three different plane rides. The doctor was very concerned about me flying because of the pain I was in and the extra pressure to my ears from the altitude. I said to her, "No, I have to go. I know the Lord will take care of me. He will heal me because He has called me to go." I went in faith. I made the flight okay. It was painful, but I made it.

The first day of the Crusade, I could barely hear. They tell me the praise and worship music was blaring, as it usually is with us, but I could barely hear the music. Usually, I am telling them to turn it down a little and this time I was struggling to hear. At the end of praise and worship, I looked up and our praise and worship leader motioned for me to come up front. I could read his lips as he called my name. I knew that the Lord was placing a Word on my heart to share, but, I thought, I can't even hear myself speak. As I began to share what the Lord had placed on my heart, it was like an echo going off in my head. I would say something and I would hear in again, but it sounded real far off. Continuing to be obedient, I began to make out the sound. All of a sudden, my ears felt like they were on fire. I knew that I was receiving *The Perfect Touch* from the Lord. He was healing my ears. Hallelujah! I began to shout, "Hallelujah! My ears are on fire, they are on fire! This is so cool! The Lord is healing me! Praise the Lord, praise the Lord!" The only ones who knew that my ears were needing healing were our team. They began to praise the Lord also. It was funny watching the audience's reaction, because they did not know what was going on. I had received *The Perfect Touch* from the Lord.

The healings that took place at that Crusade were awesome. The Lord showed up and did miraculous things. I prayed for an older lady who was suffering from memory loss, and found out later that the Lord healed her and brought back her memory. Hallelujah! The Lord also showed up and healed and delivered people from generational curses and unclean spirits. One particular lady I was praying for in the healing line was touched by the Lord right away and she went slain in the Spirit. Continuing to pray for her, the Lord spoke to me and said, "Curse and rebuke the curse that was spoken over her concerning snake oil." I began to pray that way and also against voodoo and black magic. The woman was healed of allergies and asthma that evening. At the end of the evening, her husband asked me why I spoke out about snake oil? My only comment was, "The Lord told me to. I know it sounded weird, but I spoke what He said to me."

The husband then said to me, "As a little girl, my wife's mother would anoint her with snake oil and pray for her. She would call the witch doctors over and they would pray." Wow! We have an awesome God. The lady received *The Perfect Touch* from the Lord and was not only delivered from curses, but healed.

Luke 9:37-42 *And it came to pass, that on the next day, when they were come down from the hill, much people met him. And, behold, a man of the company cried out, saying, Master, I beseech thee, look upon my son: for he is mine only child. And, lo, a spirit taketh him, and he suddenly crieth out; and it teareth him that he foameth again, and bruising him hardly departeth from him. And I besought thy disciples to cast him out; and they could not. And Jesus answering said, O faithless and perverse generation, how long shall I be with you, and suffer you? Bring thy son hither. And as he was yet a coming, the devil threw him down, and tare him. And Jesus rebuked the unclean spirit, and healed the child, and delivered him again to his father.*

Mark 1:32-34 *And at even, when the sun did set, they*

111

brought unto him all that were diseased, and them that were possessed with devils. And all the city was gathered together at the door. And he healed many that were sick of divers diseases, and cast out many devils; and suffered not the devils to speak, because they knew him.

Mark 3:9-12 *And he spake to his disciples, that a small ship should wait on him because of the multitude, lest they should throng him. For he had healed many; insomuch that they pressed upon him for to touch him, as many as had plagues. And unclean spirits, when they saw him, fell down before him, and cried, saying, Thou art the Son of God. And he straitly charged them that they should not make him known.*

When we receive a healing, there should be great joy and glory given to God. Sometimes we get our focus on the person praying for us instead of the healer, Jesus. Jesus gets all the glory!

Luke 17:11-19 *And it came to pass, as he went to Jerusalem, that he passed through the midst of Samaria and Galilee. And as he entered into a certain village, there met him ten men that were lepers, which stood afar off: And they lifted up their voices, and said, Jesus, Master, have mercy on us. And when he saw them, he said unto them, Go shew yourselves unto the priests. And it came to pass, that, as they went, they were cleansed. And one of them, when he saw that he was healed, turned back, and with a loud voice glorified God, And fell down on his face at his feet, giving him thanks: and he was a Samaritan. And Jesus answering said, Were there not ten cleansed? but where are the nine? There are not found that returned to give glory to God, save this stranger. And he said unto him, Arise, go thy way: thy faith hath made thee whole.*

Let us remember that Jesus is the one with *The Perfect Touch*, we are just the willing vessel for Him to work through. Jesus should and shall get the glory.

All of God's children, His disciples, can lay hands on the sick. All of us have the gifts of the Spirit of God if we are His children.

1 Corinthians 12:1-11 *Now concerning spiritual gifts, brethren, I would not have you ignorant. Ye know that ye were Gentiles, carried away unto these dumb idols, even as ye were led. Wherefore I give you to understand, that no man speaking by the Spirit of God calleth Jesus accursed: and that no man can say that Jesus is the Lord, but by the Holy Ghost. Now there are diversities of gifts, but the same Spirit. And there are differences of administrations, but the same Lord. And there are diversities of operations, but it is the same God which worketh all in all. But the manifestation of the Spirit is given to every man to profit withal. For to one is given by the Spirit the word of wisdom; to another the word of knowledge by the same Spirit; To another faith by the same Spirit; to another the gifts of healing by the same Spirit; To another the working of miracles; to another prophecy; to another discerning of spirits; to another divers kinds of tongues; to another the interpretation of tongues: But all these worketh that one and the selfsame Spirit, dividing to every man severally as he will.*

We should be ministering to each other in a greater way. Instead, we look at a few people whom we think only they have the anointing and expect them to heal us. Again, we all should be used as willing vessels for the Lord to work through. There is no doubt that there are great ministries out there which have a strong anointing in the healing ministry. In these last days, God is interested in all of His children being used of Him. We, as God's people, have lifted up too high those in leadership and have not taken the responsibility of what the Lord has given each one of us. We would rather others work for God instead of going to work for Him ourselves. When we say go to work for God, it starts right there in your home.

Men, you need to be the priests of your home—minister to your wife and children. Be a servant to them and pray for them when they are sick. Many get zealous to go to work for God and forget their first responsibility is in their own home. Too many get a spiritual pride. If you cannot be found faithful in your own home first, what makes you think you should be used by God outside of your home? Many ministers of God put their congregation, their preaching, teaching, and praying for others way ahead of their loved ones. When a minister of the Lord does this, a spiritual adultery takes place. This spirit causes a jealous spirit to rise up in their home. If the minister, whether it be a man or a woman, lay down their life for others before their own, rest assured that a strong jealous spirit will enter that home. When this spirit enters the home, there is hatred, envy, anger, maliciousness, strife and bitterness. A jealousy spirit will do all it can to destroy that home.

Numbers 5:11-14 *And the LORD spake unto Moses, saying, Speak unto the children of Israel, and say unto them, If any man's wife go aside, and commit a trespass against him, And a man lie with her carnally, and it be hid from the eyes of her husband, and be kept close, and she be defiled, and there be no witness against her, neither she be taken with the manner; And the spirit of jealousy come upon him, and he be jealous of his wife, and she be defiled: or if the spirit of jealousy come upon him, and he be jealous of his wife, and she be not defiled:*

James 3:16 *For where envying and strife is, there is*

confusion and every evil work.

When there is a person desiring to go to work for God
and puts his/her family down the list, there is a door that will
open up and allow a haughty spirit to come in. This spirit is a
most prideful spirit and will cause destruction. A person like
this will begin to think of themselves very highly and believes
that a red carpet should be placed about them as they walk.
With this haughty spirit, many times it opens a door for another
evil spirit. A spirit of fear will come upon the individual. They
will begin to think so highly of themselves, that they need extra
human protection. They will begin to think that someone is out
to hurt them, and that they are so well known, that not even
God can protect them. Too many times we get our focus off of
Jesus and on to our own abilities.

If you have a gift of healing and are not careful, this
haughty spirit will enter and make you think it is you, yourself,
doing all of the healing. If you have a gift of interpretation and
you think unless you are the one giving the interpretation, then
it couldn't have been right coming from someone else. Do you
begin to see the pattern? We also need to guard against the
religious spirits. In these last days there are so many
denominations and different interpretations of the Bible, along
with so many beliefs, that we have opened the door to be rigid
and unbendable in our own religious beliefs. Some Christians
believe that you should not have music, others say you should
not sing, another group believes you should not speak in tongues,
another you should only sing from hymnals, another apostles
and prophets are not for today, and another you shouldn't dance
for our King. (We will talk about praise and worship in another
chapter.) We have become unmoving in our beliefs. We have
become under the spirit of the law, staying in bondage and not
free. Where is the liberty and freedom?

If we forget who we are and leave our personalities at

home, what good are we in the church? People put on a fake personality, a facade, when they go to church. Many are trying to impress. Many are trying to put on the "Leave it to Beaver Cleavers" family. One who pretends to be the perfect family and does not need anything. They are acting perfect, when in reality they are very unhappy. There might not be any food in their cupboards, but pride and religious spirits keep them from getting the help they need. Let us pull down our fake guards and be helpers to one another. Loving one another should not be out of the question. Let us return to our freedom to worship our maker and have liberty.

If you want *The Perfect Touch* **from God, be free.**

Chapter 13

The Perfect Touch In Marriage

Marriage is like a beautiful delicate rose. The beautiful part of the rose is the color, the smell, and the soft petals. The part that can hurt are the thorns in the sides of the rose, but to make the rose more appealing, the thorns are cut off and removed from the firm stem. If the root of the rose bush is not strong, then the stems of the rose fall over. The only way to keep the rose bush producing beautiful new buds, the old petals need to be removed, cut off, and then groomed. To have The Perfect Touch from God in our marriages, we need to not bring up the past, those thorns that are stuck in our sides, we need to keep a sweet smelling savor in our marriage.

An observation that most of you will agree with; when emotions are high between the husband and wife is when most problems occur in marriage. A wise word relevant to remember during these moments; this is not a good time to "discuss" anything. As married couples find themselves during a period of a "disagreement", they allow the enemy to come in with envy, strife, and every evil work. Our flesh becomes involved and we use those thorns or daggers to throw at each other where it hurts the most. The longer you are married, you find out just where that open wound is and allow your flesh, or the enemy, to come in and try to destroy the person who is one with you. We make a decision to hurt our helpmeet, our one flesh. If there is not a decision made at that moment, to discontinue hurting your spouse, then you allow the enemy to come in and destroy what God has put together.

I am going to address marriages of Christians only, because if Jesus is not the root of your marriage, then I do not know how you can make it. It's hard enough to keep a Christian marriage going, I can't imagine going through married life without my Lord and Savior.

Statistics state there are as many divorces within the church as there are in the secular world, so we need to take a look at what is needed to save this sacred covenant, called marriage, in our lives. Our hearts are deceitful, and of course, we are the ones who always think we are right and the other is wrong.

Jeremiah 17:9-10 *The heart is deceitful above all things, and desperately wicked: who can know it? I the LORD search the heart, I try the reins, even to give every man according to his ways, and according to the fruit of his doings.*

The first thing we need to do is realize that as two people you come from two different environments. You can't control the environment you were in while growing up, but you can learn to control your tongue. What is the first thing you remember about being drawn to your mate? Was it their appearance, their personality, their income, their heart, their walk with the Lord, or do you even know? This is a question for you. The person whom I am married to today, what is the most special quality about him/her? Is it different then when you first met? Many times the thing that most attracted us to someone is the very thing that is irritating to us now. For example, if they were a person consumed with their appearance, it sometimes becomes irritating on how long it takes them to get ready. After being married for a period of time, you appreciate that they look nice, but do they have to take so long to get ready? What about an aggressive, extroverted type personality? You loved the way that they took control of the situation, and that they were the life of the party, but he/she sure can be embarrassing. On the other hand, the ones who loved how their spouse was so timid, shy, quiet and polite. Now it drives them crazy that they don't go anywhere, don't do anything, and if they do, they just sit there and people think they are rude. You see, we continue to look on the appearance of things, instead of helping each other grow and become more Christ-like in our marriages. The most powerful prayer to God comes from a married couple praying for each other. Pray for the Lord to change you and make you more like Him.

Do you need to change? When we keep Jesus in the center of our marriage and we pray that God will change ourselves to what He wants, then we can get our eyes off of the other person and the areas that need changing in them.

The aggressive extroverted type is usually the one most criticized for being most un-Christ-like. They are usually the ones who are the movers and shakers, the get-it-done type of people. Actually they have a zeal that is hard to stop and can be offensive to others. If you are that type, as you pray for the Lord to change you to be more Christ-like, a peace will come to you. You will still be that mover and shaker of the world, but you will do it with a peace and love in your heart.

If you are the shy timid kind, your focus in life is turned inward. You are self-centered and much of the time allow fear to rule your life. Many times it is this personality that tries to be so humble that actually they are very prideful. The enemy will come in and they allow their flesh to think of themselves so perfect. The whole point of these last few statements is to help you realize that not a one of us are perfect. We all need to strive to change each and every day to become more Christ-like. Jesus was a mover and a shaker. He was a hard worker. He also was the quiet type and thought deep and hard many times before He spoke. He was firm in His words, but in a loving gentle way. Jesus is calling us to be balanced. He wants us to respond to our loved ones the way He would. When we strive to be Christ-like, we are responding to His voice.

An area that most married couples do not look at before they are married is an area called rejection in their own lives. Sometimes it is fun as a young courting couple to cuddle and cry about our past. We do this because the other person is comforting and will take the time to listen. The problem is we continue to rehearse and recite the rejection in our life over and over again, just so we can feel loved and comforted by our mate. All of us, through our growing up, have gone through some kind of rejection. Obviously some have gone through greater pains than others, but the point is, we all have gone through rejection. You can't make it through life without experiencing this. If we continue to walk in our self-pity and continue to rehearse it, then our spouse can become very weary and cold to this problem which we created. Letting go of the past hurts is sometimes a most difficult thing to do. If we come into a marriage with excess baggage of hurt, unwilling to let it go and never take authority over it—never sever or loosen the rope off of us—then when we get hurt in marriage, the rope around our neck becomes tighter and tighter. Letting go the root of bitterness and hurt from our past is a must. If you have never done that totally, then now is the time to do so. Forgiveness, just like love, is a decision.

Yes, I know that the hurt may still be deep, but when you make a decision to let go of this evil thing that is holding you back from really serving the Lord to your full potential, then healing can take place. Remember, healing of the emotional wounds takes time. However, the most important thing you need to remember, is that once you let a hurt go, don't buy it back. Give it to the Lord. Trade in your sorrow for joy. Turn your mourning into laughter. There is a time for everything.

Ecclesiastes 3:1-8 *To every thing there is a season, and a time to every purpose under the heaven: A time to be born, and a time to die; a time to plant, and a time to pluck up that which is planted; A time to kill, and a time to heal; a time to break down, and a time to build up; A time to weep, and a time to laugh; a time to mourn, and a time to dance; A time to cast away stones, and a time to gather stones together; a time to embrace, and a time to refrain from embracing; A time to get, and a time to lose; a time to keep, and a time to cast away; A time to rend, and a time to sew; a time to keep silence, and a time to speak; A time to love, and a time to hate; a time of war, and a time of peace.*

After you take a look of the rejection in your life when growing up, then it is time to take a look at the rejection that has been placed in your marriage. Men, most of the time if there is a feeling of rejection from your wife, you have caused this to happen. Like it or not, God placed you at the head of the marriage, the home, the children, the finances, etc. If you, as a man, do not take responsibility to find out what it means to love your wife as Christ loves the church, then you are in for a roller coaster ride through your marriage. If you divorce, then divorce again, etc., until you find out what that means, you will continue to have a difficult marriage. Unfortunately the word "submit" is a word that many men like to misuse against the woman over and over. A man who does this never realizes his own responsibility. The scriptures also say that we are all, including men, to submit to one another.

Ephesians 5:21-31 *Submitting yourselves one to another in the fear of God. Wives, submit yourselves unto your own husbands, as unto the Lord. For the husband is the head of the wife, even as Christ is the head of the church: and he is the saviour of the body. Therefore as the church is*

121

subject unto Christ, so let the wives be to their own husbands in every thing. Husbands, love your wives, even as Christ also loved the church, and gave himself for it; That he might sanctify and cleanse it with the washing of water by the word, That he might present it to himself a glorious church, not having spot, or wrinkle, or any such thing; but that it should be holy and without blemish. So ought men to love their wives as their own bodies. He that loveth his wife loveth himself. For no man ever yet hated his own flesh; but nourisheth and cherisheth it, even as the Lord the church: For we are members of his body, of his flesh, and of his bones. For this cause shall a man leave his father and mother, and shall be joined unto his wife, and they two shall be one flesh.

Maybe this will come as a complete surprise to you men, but guess what, women are emotional! We respond to emotion. If you don't like it, then talk to God. This is how He made us.

There is one thing consistent that I have realized over the years of being married and have examined in other marriages, is that the woman is the outward appearance of the man's heart. Is the woman happy? Is she considerate? Is she kind and loving? Men in the work place; boss, husband and father, you have an awesome responsibility to treat women in your life how Christ would. She will reflect you, whether she is an employee, wife or daughter. You can tell how a marriage is going many times by just observing the wife. Men, if you don't like feeling rejected, then take a look at your life and see if there are areas that you need to change.

Early in our marriage, Stan would stay up late working on his computer. My husband is a hard worker and many times in the past, he would put his job, whether it was working for Jesus or man, first over his family. There were times I would go to bed alone at night, and cry out to the Lord, "I'll do anything, if you could just move that computer in bed with us, so at least

Stan would be in here beside me." Be careful of what you pray for, because sure enough, the Lord answered that prayer and now we have lap top computers. I must say, it wasn't long before Stan figured out that I was much softer and prettier than any computer, and gave up sitting behind that hard, cruel machine. Yea!

I believe that my husband can be a good example of what a husband should be. He came to realize that serving his family was the most important thing he could do to be the minister of the home. The more he serves us, the more we serve him. My husband doesn't serve just to get served, but submission just happens when serving is the heart of the home. Jesus was the greatest servant of all.

What does it mean to serve? In Genesis 29:20, Jacob loved Rachel and he served her father for her fourteen years. From the American Dictionary of the English Language, Noah Webster 1828, the word serve is very specific. Serve is to act as the minister of, to perform official duties to, to supply with food, to attend to, to wait on, to perform the duties required in, to be sufficient to, or to promote, to comply with, to submit to, to be in the place of anything, to obey and worship, to massage, to apply, to perform domestic offices to another, to be convenient, to officiate or minister to do the honor of.

In times past, years ago, the man came home from work and he was served. It reminds me of the Jetson's, where the husband comes home from work, the wife greets him with a kiss, the chair pulls up behind him, the child gets the slippers, and he is ready to be served. And then, all of a sudden, reality sets in and he has to go walk the dog.

Husbands if you are having a hard time getting your wife to submit, then become a servant to her. Find out what is important to her. It might be as simple as taking dirty dishes to the sink, or picking up the trail of clothes from the bathroom to the bed you left. It might be getting her that drink of water before she goes to bed at night. (Make sure you fill it to the brim with ice before placing water, in a nice sized glass for her hand to handle.) Do not worry whether she ever takes a sip of that water or not, just be a servant. As a man takes interest in his family and serves them, it causes the wife to be drawn to him. Believe me, you will be one **happy** man if you do this.

Often the woman feels as if she is the only one giving, giving, giving in the marriage. She takes care of the children, she cleans the home, she is a taxi, she washes the clothes, she has another job outside the home, she gets the children to their lessons, sports activities, school activities, gets them ready on Sunday morning, as well as you and herself, and then is expected whenever you desire, to get naked and get in bed with you. Becoming a servant means to keep or hold. Properly one that waits, stops, holds, or attends to. A person who voluntarily serves another or acts as his minister. One who yields, one who makes painful sacrifices in compliance with the weakness or wants of others. Men, I'm telling you a secret. Listen carefully! If you desire to make love to your wife whenever you desire, then be a **SERVANT!** It will work, I promise you. Through becoming Christ-like, you can have *The Perfect Touch* from your spouse.

Galatians 5:13 *For, brethren, ye have been called unto liberty; only use not liberty for an occasion to the flesh, but by love serve one another.*

Marriage is like a big ball of different colors of clay. We become all mixed together. God brings two people of different backgrounds, different personalities, different emotions and intertwines them. They become one, all connected together, but they keep their differences. But as a ball of clay goes, it is also easy to tear apart. If you were to hold a ball of clay in your hand, you can easily tear it apart, or you can continue to form the clay gently in the palm of your hand molding it, and the clay will stay connected. This is the way marriage is. It is an artwork; taking something from nothing and molding, forming, and making a beautiful design. If we allow other forces to come in and tear us apart, then we are not whole, but the good news is, we can take the torn part and stick it back together with the rest of the clay. The most important thing in marriage is; if we allow Jesus to mold us, to form us, and keep us in His big, wonderful hands, then marriage can be a beautiful creation.

Submission is a very important word in marriage as we have already discussed; however, the most important blessing in being submissive is the shield of protection. When Stan and I realized that submission was a blessing and that I was not a slave to his every demand, it was like a light bulb lighting up to both of us.

Early in our marriage, I was intimidated to call about bills. I hated calling the phone company about a problem with the bill. I hated calling about the service department to get an appointment to get the car fixed. I felt very inadequate and stupid, and it caused me to feel very insecure; however, I was to submit and make those calls because my husband told me to! Yuk! I hated that word submit. Then one day at a marriage seminar, the speaker talked about this very thing. If your wife feels insecure about doing something you have asked her to do, then men, you need to be the shield of protection for her. She is the weaker vessel. Wow! What a concept. I am the weaker vessel. If I am feeling threatened, then I can turn to my strong vessel of a man and have him take care of me. Yea! This word isn't so bad after all. As a matter of fact ladies, it is a privilege to submit. I would not want to have the responsibility that a man has. God holds him much more accountable.

Let's look at the rose again. Are there thorns in your side? Do you as a husband or wife keep prodding the sharp, painful hurt (thorn) into the other person? Remove the thorns from your marriage and don't allow them to grow back again. Be a strong stem. Become rooted in Word of God. Allow the sweet smelling savor of the Lord to be in your home. Treat each other delicately as the petals of the rose.

Men, treat your wife as if she were the weaker vessel— one who is tender and delicate. Don't try to make her a man. Don't try to make her tough and hard when she is emotional and delicate. I know, she cries a lot. She cries when she is happy. She cries when she is sad. She cries when she is mad. Men, sometimes you simply need to be that sounding board. We, as women, need a safe place to dump. Men, listen to me, we don't always want you to fix the situation. We just want to dump. You know what I mean ladies. Let's say that our boss made us mad at work and we come home upset and crying. Men, we just want to cry, complain and dump. We feel at the time that we have a right to feel this way, we feel justified in our emotional hurt, because that mean man hurt us. So what do you men do? You, the husband, the protective, mighty, strong and territorial person you are, sees that your sweet, delicate wife has been emotionally hurt, so you want to "fix" the situation. The way you want to "fix" this situation is to leave right then, go over to the boss's house and **"hurt"** the man. I mean, **"fix"** the situation. Or, are you the type who wants to pick up the phone immediately and give this boss a few words or two? Okay men, this is what women want. We don't want you to fix the problem, we just want you to be a good listener. Women need to express about three million words each day, whereas you have about fifty words you would like to share with us. You guys might as well learn to listen, because those three million words that need to come out are quickly building up day after day.

Last words of advice: Men, don't worry about trying to figure us out. We can't even figure ourselves out. It reminds me how God made Eve. The reason why men do not understand women, is that they were asleep when God created woman. Just be a good listener and treat us like the delicate part of the rose. Make the decision to serve the Lord in your household.

Ladies, don't use manipulation as a weaker vessel to get your way. We also have a responsibility to stay righteous before our King.

Joshua 24:15 ... *but as for me and my house, we will serve the LORD.*

Luke 12:37-48 *Blessed are those servants, whom the lord when he cometh shall find watching: verily I say unto you, that he shall gird himself, and make them to sit down to meat, and will come forth and serve them. And if he shall come in the second watch, or come in the third watch, and find them so, blessed are those servants. And this know, that if the goodman of the house had known what hour the thief would come, he would have watched, and not have suffered his house to be broken through. Be ye therefore ready also: for the Son of man cometh at an hour when ye think not. Then Peter said unto him, Lord, speakest thou this parable unto us, or even to all? And the Lord said, Who then is that faithful and wise steward, whom his lord shall make ruler over his household, to give them their portion of meat in due season? Blessed is that servant, whom his lord when he cometh shall find so doing. Of a truth I say unto you, that he will make him ruler over all that he hath. But and if that servant say in his heart, My lord delayeth his coming; and shall begin to beat the menservants and maidens, and to eat and drink, and to be drunken; The lord of that servant will come in a day when he looketh not for him, and at an hour when he is not aware, and will cut him in sunder, and will appoint him his portion with the unbelievers. And that servant, which knew his lord's will, and prepared not himself, neither*

127

did according to his will, shall be beaten with many stripes. But he that knew not, and did commit things worthy of stripes, shall be beaten with few stripes. For unto whomsoever much is given, of him shall be much required: and to whom men have committed much, of him they will ask the more.

Remember, allow the Lord to be that *Perfect Touch* in your marriage. Get rid of the thorns, be grounded and rooted in the Word, and treat each other like the petals. Allow the Lord to use you as *The Perfect Touch* to your spouse.

Chapter 14

Oh! The Joy

Oh Hallelujah! My favorite thing to do in the whole world, and that is to praise and worship my King! In the Bible there are 267 verses just on praise and 188 on worship alone. Obviously it is important that we praise and worship the Lord.

Psalms 22:3 *But thou art holy, O thou that inhabitest the praises of Israel.*

The Lord inhabits our praise. In other words, He shows up, He responds to us when we praise Him. Responding to the voice of the Lord through praise and worship is such an awesome experience. If you can just get to the point where in that room, it is just you and Jesus. Can you ignore others around you and experience that intimate one-to-one communication and love from our Lord? Too many times we become caught up in the cares of this world and become distracted. Even at the most wonderful praise and worship time we allow our minds to wander. Jesus is wanting to speak to you and wanting you to praise and worship Him. He doesn't just want us to praise Him because He needs it. Jesus wants us to praise Him because we need it. If you have need for joy in your life again, then praise Him and the joy of the Lord will be restored. When we praise Him then the joy of the Lord enters into us and we receive His strength.

Nehemiah 8:10 *... for this day is holy unto our Lord: neither be ye sorry; for the joy of the LORD is your strength.*

Psalms 28:7 *The LORD is my strength and my shield; my heart trusted in him, and I am helped: therefore my heart greatly rejoiceth; and with my song will I praise him.*

As we praise the Lord with music and song, then our praise for Him shall continually be in our mouths. There are many times when all night long I am praising the Lord. Sometimes I will wake up and find myself singing a praise song. When this first happened, I was wondering if I was truly getting any sleep, but each time I felt refreshed and renewed, and the most important thing was I woke up with the joy of the Lord.

He speaks to us all the time and as we send forth those words on our lips of praise to Him, we are interceding. We are doing spiritual warfare.

Psalms 33:1-2 *Rejoice in the LORD, O ye righteous: for praise is comely for the upright. Praise the LORD with harp: sing unto him with the psaltery and an instrument of ten strings.*

Psalms 34:1 *I will bless the LORD at all times: his praise shall continually be in my mouth.*

Psalms 35:18 *I will give thee thanks in the great congregation: I will praise thee among much people.*

Psalms 40:3 *And he hath put a new song in my mouth, even praise unto our God: many shall see it, and fear, and shall trust in the LORD.*

Singing and praising to the Lord is prophetic declaration and proclamation. As we respond to His voice through praise and worship, we will conquer, defeat, and triumph over the enemy in our lives if we will learn to pay attention. In Psalms

149:6, when Jehoshaphat responded to the voice of the Lord, he sent forth the singers and the praisers before the army. Why? When praise goes forth, the Lord sets ambushments against the enemy. The enemy becomes confused and is then destroyed. Hallelujah!

Psalms 149:6 *Let the high praises of God be in their mouth, and a two-edged sword in their hand;*

2 Chronicles 20:20-25 *And they rose early in the morning, and went forth into the wilderness of Tekoa: and as they went forth, Jehoshaphat stood and said, Hear me, O Judah, and ye inhabitants of Jerusalem; Believe in the LORD your God, so shall ye be established; believe his prophets, so shall ye prosper. And when he had consulted with the people, he appointed singers unto the LORD, and that should praise the beauty of holiness, as they went out before the army, and to say, Praise the LORD; for his mercy endureth for ever. And when they began to sing and to praise, the LORD set ambushments against the children of Ammon, Moab, and mount Seir, which were come against Judah; and they were smitten.*

2 Chronicles 20:27-29 *Then they returned, every man of Judah and Jerusalem, and Jehoshaphat in the forefront of them, to go again to Jerusalem with joy; for the LORD had made them to rejoice over their enemies. And they came to Jerusalem with psalteries and harps and trumpets unto the house of the LORD. And the fear of God was on all the kingdoms of those countries, when they had heard that the LORD fought against the enemies of Israel.*

Notice that before the people were to go forth and take the spoil, it was first declared unto them, "Believe in the Lord

131

your God, so shall ye be established." When the army of the Lord arrived to take the spoil of the enemy, there was so much left for them, they couldn't even carry it all. This is what the Lord does for us. As we take back what the enemy has stolen, we receive so much more than what we can even handle.

In the story of Gideon, you will see that prophetic warfare took place. There was sound, there was noise and a loud shout. The army proclaimed and pronounced the Word of the Lord. They cried with a loud shout of joy. They made a loud joyful declaration.

Judges 7:16-22 *And he divided the three hundred men into three companies, and he put a trumpet in every man's hand, with empty pitchers, and lamps within the pitchers. And he said unto them, Look on me, and do likewise: and, behold, when I come to the outside of the camp, it shall be that, as I do, so shall ye do. When I blow with a trumpet, I and all that are with me, then blow ye the trumpets also on every side of all the camp, and say, The sword of the LORD, and of Gideon. So Gideon, and the hundred men that were with him, came unto the outside of the camp in the beginning of the middle watch; and they had but newly set the watch: and they blew the trumpets, and brake the pitchers that were in their hands. And the three companies blew the trumpets, and brake the pitchers, and held the lamps in their left hands, and the trumpets in their right hands to blow withal: and they cried, The sword of the LORD, and of Gideon. And they stood every man in his place round about the camp; and all the host ran, and cried, and fled. And the three hundred blew the trumpets, and the LORD set every man's sword against his fellow, even throughout all the host: and the host fled to Bethshittah in Zererath, and to the border of Abelmeholah, unto Tabbath.*

Psalms 47:1 *O clap your hands, all ye people; shout*

unto God with the voice of triumph.

Joshua at Jericho is another example of how the voice of the Lord—the shout—the blowing of the trumpet declared victory and the walls of the enemy came tumbling down.

Joshua 6:20-21 *So the people shouted when the priests blew with the trumpets: and it came to pass, when the people heard the sound of the trumpet, and the people shouted with a great shout, that the wall fell down flat, so that the people went up into the city, every man straight before him, and they took the city. And they utterly destroyed all that was in the city, both man and woman, young and old, and ox, and sheep, and ass, with the edge of the sword.*

As we praise the Lord, our faith builds. We get strength because the joy of the Lord is our strength and the spirit of heaviness cannot stay when we praise Him. It is hard to stay depressed, oppressed and self-centered when we praise the Lord. I admit that when things in life seem to overtake me such as: deep finances, discouragement with family members, a fight with my husband or coworker, even bad hair days, broken nails, a rip or stain on my favorite outfit, a burnt dinner, or things are not going the way they should, these things will cause a distraction as I praise the Lord. The Lord wants us to set aside these distractions and get focused back on what is really important. You know, as God's children, we can pick the stupidest things in life, as well as serious mishaps, to hinder in truly praising the Lord in Spirit and in Truth.

There is healing in praising the Lord. He responds to your needs as you praise Him. The more you praise Him, the greater the boldness, strength, and joy will come to you. Try it, you'll like it! I promise!

As you come to the Lord with a cleansed pure heart you

133

will see God. Your spiritual senses will become clear, and evil will flee. With a cleansed heart you will have a clear conscience and have the right motivations and intentions. As you yearn for God, your words become loving and pure. When we realize all that our Maker has done for us each and every day, we need to make a daily habit and attitude of thankfulness. Don't stop the blessings of God coming your way through murmuring and complaining.

Thanks to our Lord starts with first recognizing that something good has been done for you. It is a daily attitude and decision. If we wait for a feeling to come first, we might never respond to the Lord. If we respond to the voice of the Lord, it then becomes possible to recognize all that He has done, and all the great and marvelous works He has done for us. Repent, begin to praise the Lord and you will become healthy in the Lord. As you praise the Lord you will begin to move out of the realm of doubt and unbelief, and into the spiritual realm of believing and faith. Don't be like the children of Israel where nothing was ever good enough. Because of their bad attitudes, complaining spirits and fearfulness, they didn't prosper and remained in the wilderness for forty years. When we praise the Lord with pure motives and being content, you will learn to enjoy the challenge and never allow defeat.

Become like a child and begin having a great time singing, lifting up your hands, dancing, clapping, shouting, spinning, leaping, and release great joy to express your gratitude to our Lord. This is true praise.

Worship is different than praise in its form and expression to the Lord. There are 188 verses in the scriptures concerning a form of worship. If we respond during worshipping our King, by kneeling or prostrating ourself, we show adoration and obedience to the Lord. To worship is loving on God and coming into the very presence of God. Worship and humbling ourselves go hand in hand. When we truly worship our Jesus, we are doing so because of our deep love for our Father. A true worshipper is a lover of God, who is genuine and sincere in developing a relationship with God. A true worshipper desires to respond to the voice of the Lord, and is led by the Holy Ghost.

Philippians 3:3 *For we are the circumcision, which worship God in the spirit, and rejoice in Christ Jesus, and have no confidence in the flesh.*

What does it mean to have no confidence in the flesh? Worshippers are not under the law or religious spirits. Worshippers are liberated—they are free. Worshippers are doers of the Word and desire to please God. A true worshipper edifies and builds up the body of Christ, and they are careful not to fall into error. Holiness becomes the greatest priority and they strive to keep a clean heart. A true worshipper can respond to the voice of the Lord because they have reverence for the Lord; they have faith, they are humble, and they first seek God. To understand worship, we need to realize that in the scriptures if someone was standing, it was usually not called worship. Standing during worship would mean disrespect in the sight of God.

1 Chronicles 29:20 *And David said to all the congregation, Now bless the LORD your God. And all the congregation blessed the LORD God of their fathers, and bowed down their heads, and worshipped the LORD, and the king.*

Exodus 34:8 *And Moses made haste, and bowed his head toward the earth, and worshipped.*

Joshua 5:14 *And he said, Nay; but as captain of the host of the LORD am I now come. And Joshua fell on his face to the earth, and did worship, and said unto him, What saith my lord unto his servant?*

1 Corinthians 14:25 *And thus are the secrets of his heart made manifest; and so falling down on his face he will worship God, and report that God is in you of a truth.*

Acts 17:25 *Neither is worshipped with men's hands, as though he needed any thing, seeing he giveth to all life, and breath, and all things;*

Exodus 33:10 *And all the people saw the cloudy pillar stand at the tabernacle door: and all the people rose up and worshipped, every man in his tent door.*

Isaiah 46:6 *They lavish gold out of the bag, and weigh silver in the balance, and hire a goldsmith; and he maketh it a god: they fall down, yea, they worship.*

Exodus 24:1 *And he said unto Moses, Come up unto the LORD, thou, and Aaron, Nadab, and Abihu, and seventy of the elders of Israel; and worship ye afar off.*

Hebrews 11:21 *By faith Jacob, when he was a dying, blessed both the sons of Joseph; and worshipped, leaning upon the top of his staff.*

Genesis 24:52 *And it came to pass, that, when Abraham's servant heard their words, he worshipped the LORD, bowing himself to the earth.*

Revelation 7:11 *And all the angels stood round about the throne, and about the elders and the four beasts, and fell before the throne on their faces, and worshipped God,*

Revelation 19:4 *And the four and twenty elders and the four beasts fell down and worshipped God that sat on the* *throne, saying, Amen; Alleluia.*

The attitude, the response of the heart is what draws us close to God with all of the love we can express. Many people find personal satisfaction in worship, but the real purpose is to draw closer to the Lord and love on the Lord. In the scriptures, Matthew 18:26-27, shows how worship opens the door for mercy on our debts.

Matthew 18:26-27 *The servant therefore fell down, and worshipped him, saying, Lord, have patience with me, and I will pay thee all. Then the lord of that servant was moved with compassion, and loosed him, and forgave him the debt.*

The way to receive *The Perfect Touch* from the Lord is truly in praising and worshipping our King. When we do this, we enter into His courtrooms of praise and He directs us. As we humble ourselves, clean up our hearts and lives, the ability to hear the Lord's voice increases. As we begin to recognize the Lord's voice, Him speaking to us, we learn to obey. Recognize that even a thought about a loved one or friend might be a message from the Lord to respond and pray. A dream that you have may be revealing the plan of the enemy in your life, in order for you to respond and do something about the devices of the devil. A vision may be a warning that needs a response, sometimes even to warn a nation. The Lord is speaking to us daily. The devil is speaking to us daily also. We need to become in tune with the Lord's voice. Pray diligently each and every day for you to respond to the voice of the Lord and a stranger you will not follow. We can all have the victory in our lives.

The Lord never desires for destruction to happen in the call He has given us. Be willing to be faithful. Be willing to persevere, to hear and respond to *The Perfect Touch* from God.

He wants His children to succeed in everything they do. If we give up too soon, or continue to walk in defeat, how can we ever learn to respond to Him? Be diligent. The Lord is for you!

Romans 8:31 *What shall we then say to these things? If God be for us, who can be against us?*

Keep the joy of the Lord! Praise on thy lips and you will receive *The Perfect Touch* from the Lord with His strength.

Chapter 15

Filter Out The Bad

Christians if you feel that you have a Word from the Lord, check your heart. Check to see if it is wisdom from above. **If you have given a Word from the Lord and feel you need to defend and prove that Word, and also to see that it is carried out, then trying to assure it is carried out, this is not from God.** Guard what is spoken because you cannot take it back. Make sure you do not listen to gossip and respond to heresay. We end up many times speaking things we should not, that are untruthful about someone because we heard someone else say it.

James 3:15-18 *This wisdom descendeth not from above, but is earthly, sensual, devilish. For where envying and strife is, there is confusion and every evil work. But the wisdom that is from above is first pure, then peaceable, gentle, and easy to be intreated, full of mercy and good fruits, without partiality, and without hypocrisy. And the fruit of righteousness is sown in peace of them that make peace.*

If someone prophesies to you, make sure you get two or three witnesses before you respond to the word spoken to you. Don't act hastily. Prophecy will divide if it is not established by two or three witnesses.

2 Corinthians 13:1 *This is the third time I am coming to you. In the mouth of two or three witnesses shall every word be established.*

139

When we get a prophetic Word from the Lord given through someone prophesying to us, we tend to run out and tell everyone. We stop everyone who will even hint that they will listen and say, "See what God is going to do in my life, see what is planned for me." We need to be ever so careful not to share that Word until two or three witnesses let it be established before mentioning it to someone else.

Also, an untimely Word to someone can be as dangerous as a wrong Word.

1 John 4:1-3 *Beloved, believe not every spirit, but try the spirits whether they are of God: because many false prophets are gone out into the world. Hereby know ye the Spirit of God: Every spirit that confesseth that Jesus Christ is come in the flesh is of God: And every spirit that confesseth not that Jesus Christ is come in the flesh is not of God: and this is that spirit of antichrist, whereof ye have heard that it should come; and even now already is it in the world.*

If you do not have peace in your heart which passeth all understanding be careful to not speak that Word to someone. If there is an exhortation for the church, but you do not have total peace, wait on the Lord. If the Word is to be spoken, God will give you the opportunity.

Philippians 4:6-7 *Be careful for nothing; but in every thing by prayer and supplication with thanksgiving let your requests be made known unto God. And the peace of God, which passeth all understanding, shall keep your hearts and minds through Christ Jesus.*

Another caution! Be careful not to get so prideful and high minded that you forget your humanness. Sometimes we Christians get too prideful and make stupid remarks. Have you ever heard the words come out of a leader, "Don't touch me, be quiet, you are going to break the anointing, or God doesn't anoint two people at the same time." Be careful of that person. The Lord is quite capable of anointing anyone He wants at any time. Also, if the anointing is there, you should not be trying to draw attention to yourself anyway. The woman with the issue of blood touched the hem of His garment. Jesus was looking around, saying who touched me? He said virtue went out of him. He did not say the anointing went out of Him.

What is virtue? Virtue is good quality or feature, effective power or force, the ability to heal or strengthen. To accept with an agreeable or positive attitude that which must be accepted anyway. Notice, it said to accept with an agreeable or positive attitude. Someone interrupting with evil intent on their heart to cause a rebuke or harm to come to a church body should not be allowed. I will emphasize! Leaders in ministry, all of us need to be careful not to bring pride into our hearts and minds. Do not become double minded. In meetings I have seen a minister, who is prophesying a Word from the Lord in front of the congregation, get upset if there is even a Hallelujah or Amen. People respond in joy when they hear a Word from the Lord—some may even begin to clap. May we, who are in ministry, realize that the anointing will not leave with a joyful response; however, we need to respond with respect and reverence to our Lord. A soft "Amen," or "Lord, let it be so," is often the response we should have. Many times people become so zealous and excited that they don't really listen to the Word from the Lord, they just clap, shout and make noise. Let's reverence our King. We need to check our hearts. Keep them pure. Remember that Jesus said "virtue" left Him—not the anointing.

There are some principles from Henry Gruver that I have learned to use and are very good to follow, especially for those newly baptized in the Holy Spirit and learning about the gifts of the Spirit. When we get the Baptism of the Holy Spirit and speak in tongues, we think we've got it. No, we didn't get it, it is that now He has us. Too many times young immature Christians begin to walk in their gifts too early. They become prideful and think they are something very spiritual, when in reality, they need to be humble and check the Spirit carefully. We all need to do this. When you are first beginning to prophesy a Word you believe is from the Lord; first, see if the Word is specific or is it vague and foggy? If it is not specific, then wait. If the Word is specific, then cover the Word given to you in the Blood of Jesus in every realm. Cover it in the Blood of Jesus to all communication coming to you, from you, around you, and concerning you. Second, keep it, but wait and begin to worship the Lord and tell Him you love Him until nothing is on your mind except the love of Jesus. Third, quiet your Spirit and see if the Lord brings it back specifically. After all three of these steps, then repeat one through three. If the word returns, then seal the word and it will not change. The Lord will watch over His Word. The Lord does desire that we respond to His voice. He wants us to prophesy; speaking unto men edification, exhortation and comfort, and the Lord wants to give you *The Perfect Touch* and respond to what He is saying to you.

I would like to close this book with this prayer. I pray all who read this book will begin to respond to the voice of the Lord.

Father, I come to you in the name of Jesus. I remit any sins from the past and all generational curses from the very first thought, word, gesture or deed, for all who pray this. I ask Lord, that if someone is praying for salvation to know you as their Lord and Savior, Master and King of their life, that you would respond with *The Perfect Touch* to them. Holy Spirit, draw them close to the Lord. I ask, Lord, that you would begin to anoint us with your *Perfect Touch* in our lives so that we will learn how to respond to your voice. I desire that all your children hear, know and respond to your voice, and your voice only. Help us to guard what comes out of our mouths. A stranger's voice we will not follow. Teach us according to your Word in Philippians. 4:6,7 that we will be careful for nothing; but in every thing by prayer and supplication with thanksgiving let your request be made known unto God. And the peace of God, which passeth all understanding, shall keep your hearts and minds through Christ Jesus.

I pray that your children will begin to know how to worship you in Spirit and in Truth. Help us to know exactly how to do this. I desire that all bondages and evil spirits that would keep your children oppressed be removed, severed, and loosed from their lives. As they put on their garments of praise for the spirit of heaviness, you would inhabit their praises. I pray that your people Lord, would begin to worship you in the way you deserve and desire. Help us to get rid of all hindrances, inhibitions, distractions and pride so that we can truly reverence you most Holy King. I pray in the name of Jesus that you would begin to show confirmations to us as we pray. Help us to see these confirmations so that our faith would increase. Give us, your people, a special gift of faith whether we are in a time of blessing or despair. You are an awesome God and we praise your most Holy Name.

I love you Lord with all my body, soul, and spirit. I love you Lord with all the praise and worship I can exhibit. Take us to your holy of holies and enter into the courtrooms of praise so that we can truly honor and exalt your name. Lord, as it says in a worship song to you, "like a rose trampled on the ground, you took the fall, and thought of me, above all". You are not a trampled rose anymore. You are that sweet smelling rose. The perfect rose. The Savior which is alive, who died and rose again for our sins. Thank you, Lord, for responding to your people and the blessings you bestow upon us with your touch, *The Perfect Touch.* In Jesus Name, Amen!

Remember, Jesus is the filter. He is the one who cleanses us all from unrighteousness. Jesus is *The Perfect Touch* !

For more information concerning the following:

- Additional copies of this book
- Schedule speaking engagements
- The radio program, *The Perfect Touch*
- ***The Power of Jesus Crusades!***

You may contact Leslie at:

Leslie Johnson
c/o Spirit of Prophecy Church
P. O. Box 750234
Topeka, KS   66675

e-mail: lesliej@cjnetworks.com
or
Phone: 785/266-1112
Fax: 785/266-6200